HOW TO STUDY LITERATURE
General Editors: John Peck and Martin Coyle

HOW TO BEGIN STUDYING ENGLISH LITERATURE

Second Edition

IN THE SAME SERIES

How to Begin Studying English Literature*   *Nicholas Marsh*
How to Study a Jane Austen Novel   *Vivien Jones*
How to Study Chaucer   *Robert Pope*
How to Study a Joseph Conrad Novel   *Brian Spittles*
How to Study a Charles Dickens Novel   *Keith Selby*
How to Study an E. M. Forster Novel   *Nigel Messenger*
How to Study a Thomas Hardy Novel   *John Peck*
How to Study a D. H. Lawrence Novel   *Nigel Messenger*
How to Study Milton   *David Kearns*
How to Study a Novel*   *John Peck*
How to Study a Shakespeare Play*   *John Peck and Martin Coyle*
How to Study Modern Drama   *Kenneth Pickering*
How to Study Modern Poetry   *Tony Curtis*
How to Study a Poet   *John Peck*
How to Study a Renaissance Play   *Chris Coles*
How to Study Romantic Poetry   *Paul O'Flinn*
Literary Terms and Criticism*   *John Peck and Martin Coyle*
Practical Criticism   *John Peck and Martin Coyle*

Now in a second edition

Series Standing Order

If you would like to receive future titles in this series as they are published, you can make use of our standing order facility. To place a standing order please contact your bookseller or, in case of difficulty, write to us at the address below with your name and address and the name of the series. Please state with which title you wish to begin your standing order. (If you live outside the UK we may not have the rights for your area, in which case we will forward your order to the publisher concerned.)

Standing Order Service, Macmillan Distribution Ltd,
Houndmills, Basingstoke, Hampshire, RG21 2XS, England

HOW TO BEGIN STUDYING ENGLISH LITERATURE

Second Edition

Nicholas Marsh

MACMILLAN

First edition 1987
Reprinted five times
Second edition 1995

Published by
MACMILLAN PRESS LTD
Houndmills, Basingstoke, Hampshire RG21 2XS
and London
Companies and representatives
throughout the world

ISBN 0-333-64090-X

A catalogue record for this book is available
from the British Library.

10   9   8   7   6   5   4   3   2   1
04   03   02   01   00   99   98   97   96   95

Typeset by Acorn Bookwork, Salisbury, Wiltshire

Printed in Malaysia

For Simon

Contents

General editors' preface

EVERYBODY who studies literature, either for an examination or simply for pleasure, experiences the same problem: how to understand and respond to the text. As every student of literature knows, it is perfectly possible to read a book over and over again and yet still feel baffled and at a loss as to what to say about it. One answer to this problem, of course, is to accept someone else's view of the text, but how much more rewarding it would be if you could work out your own critical response to any book you choose or are required to study.

The aim of this series is to help you develop your critical skills by offering practical advice about how to read, understand and analyse literature. Each volume provides you with a clear method of study so that you can see how to set about tackling texts on your own. While the authors of each volume approach the problem in a different way, every book in the series attempts to provide you with some broad ideas about the kind of texts you are likely to be studying and some broad ideas about how to think about literature; each volume then shows you how to apply these ideas in a way which should help you construct your own analysis and interpretation. Unlike most critical books, therefore, the books in this series do not simply convey someone else's thinking about a text, but encourage you and show you how to think about a text for yourself.

Each book is written with an awareness that you are likely to be preparing for an examination, and therefore practical advice is given not only on how to understand and analyse literature, but also on how to organise a written response. Our hope is that although these books are intended to serve a practical purpose, they may also enrich your enjoyment of literature by making you a more confident reader, alert to the interest and pleasure to be derived from literary texts.

John Peck
Martin Coyle

1

Finding a theme

MAKING A START

THE first problem every student of literature faces is a feeling of blankness. I have read the text, now I am supposed to study it: how do I start? Teachers and critics sometimes make this stage more difficult by pretending that literature is a special subject which only experts can understand. Nothing could be more misleading. Great writers and poets write because they want to communicate with ordinary readers like you and me: they do not write for experts. They are not writing on a specialised subject, either. Literature is about the same things you and I are concerned with: life and living. Be confident, therefore. Every student finds the first step in studying literature difficult, but there is nothing mysterious or specialised about it. The difficulty you face at the beginning is simply one of choosing what to focus on out of the rich mass of details, characters, events and so on, which you have met in reading the text. You are faced with the intricate complexity of a literary work: as soon as you can decide what to study first, and where to start, you can make a start.

What will obviously help you is if you have a method which tells you how and where to start. The method I will be explaining in this book can be applied to any of the texts you have to study, whether they are novels, plays or poems. I shall be showing how you can think about the text, and go on to study important passages, so your understanding develops fruitfully and is supported by the detailed analysis you need when you come to write essays or examinations. The way to overcome the first difficulty is really quite straightforward: you can make a start by finding a theme.

WHAT IS A THEME?

A theme is simply this: a subject which interests the writer, and which is discussed in the text or portrayed in it in some way. Finding a 'subject' in a book may sound difficult, but when you know the kind of subject you are looking for you will see that it is quite easy. A theme is not a summary of the story: that is not what the text is 'about'; nor is it a special subject you have to search for. Literature is about ordinary life, so the big themes in literature are the important subjects and experiences of our public and private lives: they are the ordinary and common words in our everyday thoughts and conversations, like love, death, marriage, freedom, hope, despair, power, war, revenge, evil, and so on. This list of the big common experiences of life could go on and on, because anything which is a subject in life can become a theme in literature. The first thing you can say about a text is that it is about one of these common subjects, so the first thing you say is startlingly simple. You might think it even too obvious, but it is a very important step forward because you have left the feeling of blankness behind: you simply say 'There is a lot in it about love', or 'It is about hope and despair'. Then you have made a start.

There is one more point to make about themes. They are big ordinary subjects, but they are complex. The texts you study focus on the problems people face, their contradictory feelings, and the complex moral and social entanglements which confront people and make our experience of living so complex. So the big ideas in a text are not simple opinions: they are full of complexity like our experience of life itself.

CHOOSING A PASSAGE TO STUDY

The writer weaves his themes into every aspect of the life of the text. Because these major concerns are portrayed throughout the text, you still have the problem of choosing a part to look at more closely. What is more, the part you choose must be short enough for you to think about without confusion; at the same time, it must be important enough to reveal something significant about the text when you study it. How can you be sure of choosing an important passage, which will be really revealing to study? The answer is to look for a *crisis* in the text. A crisis is a place where there is a sudden event like a murder or a wedding or a confession or a quarrel or a battle. In a crisis there is sudden action or change. It shakes up the life of the text, so the feelings, ideas and important issues are thrown into particularly sharp relief. In a crisis, then, the big issues are portrayed most openly and forcefully, so choosing a crisis to study will tell you a lot about the text as a whole.

It is worth pausing at this stage to gain a clearer idea of how the crises in life and literature happen. All the big labels we use for themes or feelings stand for complex experiences: they are made up of many different elements. For example, the big label 'love' may stand for a mixture of feelings including admiration, lust, or even fear or hatred. These different feelings and ideas manage to rub along together most of the time, so our lives are usually fairly calm. In a crisis, however, something puts the complex mixture under pressure, upsetting its balance and making its different elements struggle against each other in conflict. The tensions and worries which are usually kept under control are therefore brought to the surface in a crisis. In a novel, for example, a character might have feelings of love and jealousy about his wife, but they live happily together because his jealousy is under control. Suddenly he has to go away without his wife, and the pressure of separation makes his jealousy grow out of proportion. When he comes home he questions her suspiciously, they argue and he hits her. Their life will never be the same again. Notice that this character had complex jealous feelings all the time, but it was the extra pressure of being away which brought about a crisis, making his feelings lose balance and explode into sudden and revealing action.

Look for the crises in the text you have to study, then, because the crises are places where the themes and everything else about the text come out into the open. Again, however, try to make your choice logically: look for the kind of crisis that will tell you about the theme you have already found. Think about the theme and choose a crisis which is bound to be about that theme. For example, if you have found a theme of love, look for a crisis about love. What are the sudden and drastic things that happen to lovers? Look for proposals of marriage, weddings, quarrels, separations, the death of a loved one, betrayals of love. If you have found a theme of war, look for the most important or shattering things that happen in war: battles, an armistice, a character's first experience of action, or a character being wounded or killed. Choose a theme first, then think about it so you can choose what sort of crisis is likely to bring out that big issue most directly and forcefully.

HOW TO STUDY

I have said quite a lot about how you can make a start in studying a text. The two main points you should grasp to see the logic of this approach are that themes are big ordinary subjects in life, and that life throws up sudden crises which are revealing. If you are still unsure how these ideas are going to work when you actually try to use them, do not worry: in the rest of this chapter I will be showing how to apply them in detailed, step-by-step examples. Before we move on to the examples, however, here is a brief summary of the three logical steps in studying that I am going to apply to the examples throughout this book.

1 *Think about the text*

This is the step I have been describing already. When you have finished reading a text, think about it and ask yourself what common experiences it is dealing with: is it about love, war, marriage or revenge? Then choose a crisis passage from the text to look at more closely. By thinking logically and positively, use this step to help you overcome the first problem and find a way into understanding the text.

2 *Analyse the text*

You have chosen an important short passage from the text. Now look at it closely, analysing in detail to see exactly how it portrays the theme or other aspect you are studying. In this step your ideas become more precise and detailed because you concentrate on finding the complexity of different elements which make up the major theme you are interested in. This step also gives you the kind of exact evidence you will need to support your ideas when you come to write essays.

3 *Relate the part you have studied to the text as a whole*

Finally, work out how the part you have studied in detail fits into the work as a whole. This step should confirm that the detailed ideas you have found are an important part of the text as a whole; and because you broaden your outlook again, you develop an understanding of how the complexity of the theme lives and develops through the whole extent of the text.

All three steps are necessary. You have to make decisions about what is important at first, or you will be left in confusion asking 'How can I start?' You must analyse a part of the text in detail to make your ideas precise, and to make sure your arguments are sound and well-supported so your essays will stand up to an examiner's scrutiny. You have to relate your detailed study to the whole text, or you may be stuck with only a narrow or partial understanding. Like a machine, a book will only work when all its bits and pieces are working together; so you will only fully understand the part you are concentrating on when you fit it into its place in the whole text. The three steps I have described can be used to examine every aspect of a text, and any kind of text. Indeed, the examples which make up the rest of this chapter show how to apply them to both a long, complicated novel, and a short poem.

Wuthering Heights by Emily Brontë

1 *Think about the text*

This first example shows how to find and study a major theme in a long, complicated text. *Wuthering Heights* is a 400-page novel crowded with events which span two generations of two families. Here is a brief summary of the plot, so that you can imagine you have read the novel and are just starting to study it.

Mr Earnshaw, owner of Wuthering Heights, brings home and adopts a beggar-boy he found wandering the streets, and calls him Heathcliff. Mr Earnshaw's two children, Hindley and Catherine, react very differently to the boy. Catherine becomes very close to Heathcliff and they are constant companions, while Hindley is jealous and hates the newcomer. When Mr Earnshaw dies, Hindley becomes master of Wuthering Heights and uses his new power to revenge himself on Heathcliff by separating him from Catherine and making him live as a servant. Heathcliff runs away. When he returns three years later he finds Catherine already married to the rich Edgar Linton and sets about taking his revenge on Hindley, Catherine and Edgar. First, he marries Edgar's sister Isabella to spite Catherine. Catherine herself dies in childbirth, leaving a daughter, also called Catherine. Heathcliff continues his revenge by becoming the master of Wuthering Heights. He brings up Hareton, Hindley's son, to be an illiterate labourer, and completes his revenge by kidnapping and blackmailing young Catherine into marrying his own sickly son Linton, thus making sure he will be master of the Lintons' property as well. Isabella is dead, having run away from Heathcliff, Edgar Linton dies, Hindley dies, and the sickly boy Linton dies. Eventually Heathcliff also dies after being haunted for years by the ghost of the Catherine he loved but never married. At the end of the book Hareton (Hindley's son) and young Catherine fall in love, and happiness returns to Wuthering Heights.

This is the barest outline of the story, but as you can tell it is a very complicated plot. The problem of starting to study is at its most difficult here: there are several relationships, several characters and a lot of incidents. Given such complications, how can you choose where to start in your study of the text? Remember, first of all, that you cannot explain the whole text at once. In most of the texts you study you are likely to find several main themes, but for now I only want to find one so that I can make a start. Secondly, you are studying so that you will eventually be able to write essays on the text. This means that you have to find a theme and equip yourself with some close under-standing of how it is portrayed in the text, and you have to find evi-dence, that is, quotations and close references, which show how the theme is portrayed. However, you do not need to trace the theme through the whole text. Set your sights realistically: you cannot explain the whole text at once, so find a theme and then choose a part of the text to look at more closely.

Start by considering the story as a whole. What sort of a story is *Wuthering Heights*? It is not about war, or politics, or learning or travel-ling. It is a love story: the plot depends on marriages, relationships between men and women, jealousies and betrayals of love. I have now found a theme, because I can make a statement about *Wuthering Heights*: there is a lot in it about love. I have already warned you that the first move in studying might seem too obvious to be worthwhile. Remem-ber, however, that it is a very important move because I no longer face the endless complications of the whole of the text. Now we are only dealing with one subject: love.

The next task is to find a crisis which is about love. A crisis is a place where events and feelings come together into a sudden or violent experience which changes the plot and characters. I want to find a crisis which will portray the theme of love, so I begin by thinking about love to work out the kind of crisis I am looking for. In this case, events like the death of a lover, a wedding, a quarrel between lovers, or a separation of lovers, would all be crises likely to tell me about how love is shown in the text. If you had just finished reading *Wuthering Heights*, you would have a choice of several episodes which are crises about love. I have chosen a quarrel between young Catherine and Hareton, which occurs near the end of the story. I am going to look at this quarrel in detail in order to discover how Emily Brontë portrays the theme of love in this crisis. Now I have completed Step 1: I have found a theme by thinking about the story and by saying there is a lot in the text about love; and I have chosen Catherine and Hareton's quarrel near the end as a crisis to look at in more detail.

2 *Analyse the text*

The first task in this step is to reread the crisis you have chosen to analyse. Here is an outline of the quarrel I have chosen to study. Catherine and Hareton quarrel in Chapter 31 over Hareton's attempt to learn how to read. Catherine discovers that he has stolen some of her books, and she ridicules his illiteracy. She teases him until he hits her, throws the books on the fire and rushes out. In the next chapter Hareton is sulking, and Catherine wants to be friends with him. She tries to charm him into speaking to her and talks to the servant Nellie about how she wants to be friends with Hareton. Eventually she kisses Hareton when he does not expect it, makes a parcel of some books as a present for him, and promises to teach him how to read. Catherine gradually overcomes Hareton's resentful mood, particularly when she unexpectedly kisses him.

Notice that this outline is much more detailed than my original overall summary, because I have narrowed down what I am looking at by choosing their quarrel as an important crisis. The task of analysing two chapters in detail is still too large, however, so use the same method again to narrow your focus. When you have reread the whole of the crisis scene, look for crises or 'turning-points' within it. You need to find short passages which describe the actual moments when something decisive happens. When Catherine and Hareton quarrel, their argument builds up as Catherine teases him, and the crisis in the scene occurs when Hareton loses his temper and hits her. When they are reconciled in the next chapter, Catherine tries and tries to make friends with him, but the 'turning-point' is only reached when she kisses him. Now I have narrowed down the search even further, so I can focus on two short passages from the text.

You may feel worried when you reach this stage in case you are missing too much by devoting your attention to such short passages. The method we are using, however, focuses on the most significant moments, when the feelings and ideas of the text explode out into the open. In addition, you will find that even the shortest passages provide rich and complex material for analysis, so there is plenty you can discover from them.

Here, then, is the first of my two passages, where the narrator tells how Hareton loses his temper in their quarrel:

> But his self-love would endure no further torment: I heard, and not altogether disapprovingly, a manual check given to her saucy tongue. The little wretch had done her utmost to hurt her cousin's sensitive though uncultivated feelings, and a physical argument was the only mode he had of balancing the account and repaying its effects on the inflicter. He afterwards gathered the books and hurled them on the fire. I read in his countenance what anguish it was to offer that sacrifice to spleen – I fancied that as they consumed, he recalled the pleasure they had already imparted, and the triumph and ever-increasing pleasure he had anticipated from them; and I fancied I guessed the incitement to his secret studies, also. He had been content with daily labour and rough animal enjoyments, till Catherine crossed his path. Shame at her scorn, and hope of her approval, were his first prompters to higher pursuits; and instead of guarding him from one, and winning him the other, his endeavours to raise himself had produced just the contrary result.
>
> (*Wuthering Heights*, Penguin, 1979, p. 333)

I am investigating the theme of love in *Wuthering Heights*, so I need to look at the way love is portrayed here. One thing that is clear is that this passage does not have anything to say about tenderness or affection, and you may be put off at first, thinking it has nothing to do with love. Remember, however, that I have chosen this short passage logically because it is the crisis of their quarrel. Be confident, therefore, and keep an open mind. Love is the emotional relationship between these two characters. Look at the passage: what do Catherine and Hareton feel? What particular kinds of emotion are brought out here that link these two characters' hearts together? It seems to me that the passage brings out how Catherine and Hareton can hurt each other. She can use her superior education to hurt him by teasing him about not being able to read; and he hurts her in the only way he can, by hitting her. The narrator makes this clear: 'a physical argument was the only mode he had of balancing the account'. What we also learn from the passage is that Hareton is in 'anguish'. The first sentence tells of his 'torment', while the rest of the passage dwells on how much Catherine's 'scorn' and 'approval' matter to him. All these painful feelings, however, are connected with love: Hareton suffers because he has fallen in love. So, looking at the feelings in this passage, I can say that love is portrayed as something painful, as a sort of mental torment.

Here is the second of my short passages, the crisis in their reconciliation. Catherine has been begging Hareton to be her friend, but he answers angrily, and is determined not to let himself be scorned again, declaring, 'Nay, if it made me a king, I'd not be scorned for seeking her good will any more'. Catherine, however, begs him to forgive her:

> She returned to the hearth, and frankly extended her hand. He blackened, and scowled like a thunder-cloud, and kept his fists resolutely clenched, and his gaze fixed on the ground.
> Catherine, by instinct, must have divined it was obdurate perversity, and not dislike, that prompted this dogged conduct; for, after remaining an instant undecided, she stooped, and impressed on his cheek a gentle kiss. The little rogue thought I had not seen her, and, drawing back, she took her former station by the window quite demurely. I shook my head reprovingly; and then she blushed, and whispered –
> 'Well! what should I have done, Ellen? He wouldn't shake hands, and he wouldn't look: I must show him some way that I like him – that I want to be friends.'
> Whether the kiss convinced Hareton, I cannot tell: he was very careful, for some minutes, that his face should not be seen; and when he did raise it, he was sadly puzzled where to turn his eyes.
>
> (pp. 344–5)

The theme I am studying is love, so I must again look at the feelings described in the passage. This passage tells us more about Catherine's feelings. The writer describes how Catherine is at first 'undecided', but then 'divined' the truth by 'instinct'. She had talked to Hareton, apologised to him, cried, and held out her hand, but to no avail. By instinct, however, she kisses him. She feels forced to go further and further because, as she says, 'I must show him some way that I like him'. In other words, Catherine's instinctive feelings make her go beyond all the normal and reasonable ways of settling a quarrel. Hareton rejects all her advances, but her feelings are so strong that she has to go further, and her feelings also show her, by a sort of 'instinct' which can 'divine' Hareton's heart, exactly the right and only way to show Hareton that she cares. Love in this passage, then, is presented as a powerful irrational instinct which drives people to break down all the barriers in their way until they are united with the loved one. This may seem strong language for one kiss, but Catherine's blush and excuse and the narrator's reaction show that she acts beyond the expected range of behaviour.

I have now examined two passages in detail, asking in each case what they tell me about love in *Wuthering Heights*. From analysing the text, I have learned two important points about the theme of love. First, people who are in love are vulnerable: they can be hurt and tortured because they are in love. Secondly, when love works to bring people together, it does not respect any restraints: it acts as an 'instinct' determined to go beyond all conventions in uniting the lovers. I found these two points because Hareton suffers so painfully from being in love, and because Catherine perseveres in breaking down Hareton's mood and being reconciled even after he has rejected all her apologies and advances.

I have now finished the second step. Notice that in this step I have moved closer and closer to the actual text, focusing gradually on the significant details even to the point of a few phrases and words, such as 'anguish', 'torment' and 'instinct'. You have to go into this sort of close reading in this step in order to give your ideas precision and gain the detailed evidence you will need for your essays. Do not worry about narrowing down your study in this way, because the short passages we focused on in this step were chosen as part of a crisis: in other words we deliberately chose an especially revealing part of the text to *discover points that are important throughout the work*. This is why you can move on to Step 3 confidently, and discover how your detailed analysis of the crisis fits in with the rest of the text. You have found out a lot in Step 2 because you have come to grips with the central complexities of the theme you are studying.

3 *Relate the part you have studied to the text as a whole*

In the first two steps my study of *Wuthering Heights* has narrowed down from thinking about the whole story to analysing a few words. Now the study becomes broad again, for in this step you look at the text as a whole. When you study literature you are expected to do something called 'developing your ideas'. This means using what you know to find out about what you do not know yet. Studying a text is not just a matter of collecting more and more facts: your ideas actually grow and develop as you pursue them through further areas of the text. You can do this by turning what you know into the kind of question which will lead you to a fuller understanding of the text, and in the course of this book I will be showing you how to work out the right questions to ask. Sometimes you might feel that these questions are too obvious, too much like common sense to be proper academic work. Literature is about ordinary life, however, and it is written for ordinary readers like you or me, so you must not underrate the value of common sense or ignore the obvious. Asking the obvious question to develop your ideas is a very important move forward. When you have found a theme and analysed how it is portrayed in a crisis, there are two clear questions to ask about the rest of the text. First, are the points I have discovered in this crisis important in the rest of the text and, second, have I found out all there is to find about the theme or does it run much deeper and go further than I have discovered from just one crisis?

In my case, I have found two specific points about love as a theme of *Wuthering Heights*: that love causes suffering and is a kind of mental torment; and that it is an instinct which drives people to break down conventional barriers so they can be united with the person they love. In Step 3, look at other crises which are to do with your theme, and look for the points you have already found to see if they are repeated elsewhere in the text. This will answer the first question and confirm that what you have discovered is important in the text as a whole; it will also develop your ideas, because the theme gains breadth and power as it is revealed in different ways in different contexts.

In Step 3, then, use the same method again. Choose other crises about love from the text, and reread them. This time, however, you have an advantage because you bring with you your understanding of the first crisis you looked at. You do not need to start again with just the idea of love: now you can look at love in terms of suffering and how love throws down all barriers and restraints.

In *Wuthering Heights* the most important lovers are the elder Catherine and Heathcliff. Here are passages from two of the crises of their love: the first comes from a scene when they quarrel about Heathcliff's plan to marry Isabella; the second describes Catherine's illness and delirium after she has quarrelled with both Heathcliff and her husband Edgar. Catherine and Heathcliff quarrel because he is planning to marry Isabella as part of his revenge, and Catherine knows he does not

love Isabella. When I reread this quarrel, I found this speech from
Heathcliff describing the torture and pain of their love:

> 'I seek no revenge on you,' replied Heathcliff less vehemently. 'That's not
> the plan. The tyrant grinds down his slaves and they don't turn against
> him; they crush those beneath them. You are welcome to torture me to
> death for your amusement, only allow me to amuse myself a little in the
> same style, and refrain from insult as much as you are able. Having level-
> led my palace, don't erect a hovel and complacently admire your own
> charity in giving me that for a home. If I imagined you really wished me
> to marry Isabella, I'd cut my throat!'
>
> (p. 151)

This speech shows that the idea of lovers torturing each other is again
very strong in the novel: love here is portrayed in terms of anguish,
torment and suffering, so I know that the first point I noticed about
Hareton is an important part of the pattern of the text. Heathcliff sees
Catherine as a 'tyrant' who 'grinds' him down, making him a 'slave'.
At the same time we see that Heathcliff intends to hurt her, by making
her jealous of Isabella. He says he would kill himself if he thought he
could not make Catherine suffer. Notice that this passage conveys a
much stronger sense of suffering and torture than in the first crisis we
looked at: Hareton slapped his love and threw books into the fire, but
Heathcliff says that love, with all its pain, is worth more to him than
life; he would cut his throat if he did not have this tortuous relationship
to live for.

After quarreling with Edgar, Catherine locks herself in her room
and stays there without eating for three days. When the servant Nellie
goes in she finds Catherine in a delirium. Rereading this episode, I
found the following speech from Catherine, which not only shows how
far she will go to be reunited with Heathcliff, but also how much she
demands of him in return. In her delirium Catherine talks to Heathcliff, although he is not actually there:

> 'It's a rough journey, and a sad heart to travel it; and we must pass by
> Gimmerton Kirk, to go that journey! We've braved its ghosts often toge-
> ther, and dared each other to stand among the graves and ask them to
> come . . . But Heathcliff, if I dare you now, will you venture? If you do,
> I'll keep you. I'll not lie there by myself: they may bury me twelve feet
> deep, and throw the church down over me, but I won't rest till you are
> with me. I never will!'
>
> (p. 164)

In this speech Catherine dares Heathcliff to die for her so they can lie together at last in their graves in the churchyard, once more stressing the idea that love breaks down all restraints and makes extraordinary demands.

The two crises I have looked at in Step 3 reveal the same two points about love that I discovered from the quarrel I originally analysed in Step 2, and the importance of these ideas and the theme of love in the text as a whole is confirmed. In addition, these extracts have strengthened and added to what I know. Catherine threw aside conventional polite behaviour when she kissed Hareton because apologies were not enough. The same idea of going to extraordinary lengths comes up in the elder Catherine's demand that Heathcliff should die for her, but this time the sacrifice is life itself. So I can develop what I can say about love: it not only demands more than is expected, but there is no limit to what love will demand – even death. Indeed, love is now shown to be more important than death or life to both Catherine and Heathcliff.

Notice that the ideas I held at the beginning of Step 3 have been confirmed and strengthened. Step 3 has done more than merely confirm two points, however: it has helped me to gain a broader and unified understanding of the theme. I looked at short passages and found complex elements, but this has helped me, now, to gain a larger understanding of the theme as it is presented in the whole wide sweep of the text: love is shown as a force which is irresistible, more powerful than life or death. The two points I found – that love contains extreme suffering and extreme desire – can now be understood as part of the single big subject, the overwhelming power of love in *Wuthering Heights*.

This third step, then, confirms the significance of the theme and what you have found out about it, but also adds to your ideas, enabling you to develop them further and bringing you to a sense of the overall forceful presentation of the theme in the whole text. The method of analysis I have described here has begun to convey a sense of what the novel is about, and I can appreciate the depth and scope of ideas about love which are shown in the lives and experiences of Brontë's characters. The same method can be applied to all your texts: it will help you to look at any text in a structured and fruitful way. In order to further illustrate this I now want to turn from a long, complicated novel to a short poem.

'Do Not Go Gentle into That Good Night' by Dylan Thomas

1 *Think about the text*

Plays, novels and narrative poems have a story and characters whom you know as soon as you have read the text. When you study short poems you are faced with a different problem because they do not usually have a story. There are no events, people or places in a short poem, there is no ordinary life happening which you can get hold of when you read it for the first time. Instead, a poem seems like a fragment or crisis from the middle of a story. Approaching poems this way can be helpful: when you read a poem, remember the idea of a crisis, a sudden event that shakes up the balance of ordinary life, and this will help you start to understand the poem.

Most short poems do, in fact, just focus on a crisis, on a sudden explosion of action and change in life. Think of a poem as a crisis from an unwritten story. A poem is a moment of intense feeling or heightened thought expressing sudden important feelings or a new way of looking at the world, so it is an important fragment taken from life. It follows that there was a background which led up to the poem, just as the story of a longer text leads up to the crisis. The difference is that a novelist or a playwright tells us the background story, and a poet does not: he gives us the crisis on its own.

This is one of the reasons why students find poetry more confusing and baffling than longer texts: and you may feel annoyed and wonder why poets play games and hide their meaning. They are not playing games with you, of course: the poet leaves out the background story because he wants to communicate powerful feelings and ideas in a very purified form. Poets, however, do want us to understand what they are saying and so they put enough information into the poem to enable us to work out what is happening. There are always clues about the background story in a poem. They are not detailed and not like a full narrative, but the poet does make sure that the essential information about the situation which produced the poem is there for us to understand.

The first thing to do in studying a poem, then, is to reconstruct the situation which led up to or produced the poem. This will put you in the same position as when you start to study a novel or a play: it will tell you all you need to know so you can find a theme. You will not find the poem's story in the poet's biography, however. Many students make the mistake of studying the poet instead of studying the poem. Remember that the text itself is your subject, and other historical or biographical information you might read is only secondary. Concentrate only on the poem, then, and try to find out what was happening when the poem was written.

There are three particular questions you can use which will help you to reconstruct the situation behind the poem. First, **in what** circumstances was the poem written? For example, the poem may have been written after the poet's first taste of battle in a war, or when he had just fallen in love. Second, **to whom is the poem addressed?** Most poems are addressed directly to the reader, but many are addressed to lovers, wives, husbands, the poor, kings, gods, or a dead friend. Third, **what is the main thing the poem expresses?** When answering this question, stick to simple statements about the poem: your answer might be as short as one word. For example, the poem may express love, disillusionment or ecstasy. You can use these questions to help you approach any poem. Do not allow yourself to be baffled by the poem. Take the same attitude as I suggested with longer texts: do not expect to understand the whole poem in one go. Any fragment of information you can get hold of about the poem's background situation is something to build on and gives you a way in. I will give you more hints on approaching poetry in later chapters, but keeping an open mind and asking these three questions will give you a good start. The secret is not to expect too much too soon but, as in the discussion below, try to build your response carefully and logically. My example is a poem by Dylan Thomas called 'Do Not Go Gentle into That Good Night':

Do not go gentle into that good night,
Old age should burn and rave at close of day;
Rage, rage against the dying of the light.

Though wise men at their end know dark is right,
Because their words had forked no lightning they
Do not go gentle into that good night.

Good men, the last wave by, crying how bright
Their frail deeds might have danced in a green bay,
Rage, rage against the dying of the light.

Wild men, who caught and sang the sun in flight,
And learn, too late, they grieved it on its way,
Do not go gentle into that good night.

Grave men, near death, who see with blinding sight
Blind eyes could blaze like meteors and be gay,
Rage, rage against the dying of the light.

And you, my father, there on the sad height,
Curse, bless, me now with your fierce tears, I pray.
Do not go gentle into that good night.
Rage, rage against the dying of the light.

(from *Nine Modern Poets*, Macmillan, 1975, p. 148)

When you have read the poem, write a summary of the background situation, answering as best you can the three questions I listed above. The poem you are studying may not give an answer to all three of these questions, but an answer to just one of them will be enough to give you a start: you will have found a way in, however small and unimportant it might seem at first. It is useful to write a summary of the background situation, because thinking about your summary will be easier than trying to think about the whole text. Remember, the three questions you are trying to answer are: in what circumstances was the poem written, to whom is it addressed and what does it express?

This is how I see the background situation of 'Do Not Go Gentle into That Good Night': in line 4 I notice that 'wise men' are said to be 'at their end' and in line 13 'grave men' are 'near death'. Dylan Thomas's father is apparently in the same situation as these others because the poet says in line 16 he is 'there on that sad height', and I notice that he gives his father the same advice he gave to the other people mentioned in the poem. I have, then, found out the circumstances in which this poem came to be written and answered the first question: the poet's father was dying when he wrote this poem.

To whom is the poem addressed? I can find the answer to this question in line 16, where the poet writes 'and you, my father': it is written to his dying father. Finally, what is the main thing the poem expresses? I already know that his father and the other people mentioned are all near death; and the repeated lines 'Do not go gentle into that good night' and 'Rage, rage against the dying of the light' are commands: Dylan Thomas is telling his father and other people what to do when they are dying. The idea that light is life and death is darkness is therefore clear. I can work out that 'the dying of the light' and 'that good night' both stand for death. So this poem expresses feelings about death. This summary is enough to give a way into the poem, because I have found the essential information which helps me to understand that the poem is a crisis. There is no difficulty in understanding that his father's death was an emotional crisis in the poet's life.

At this stage you are at the same point as when you begin studying a play or a novel: you now know the 'story' of the poem. The next thing to do, therefore, is to think about that story until you find a major theme, a big ordinary subject which is part of everyone's experience. In this poem, the theme of death stands out as the obvious big subject, so naturally I will choose death as the theme to study. I have now completed Step 1: I have described the poem's situation, finding answers to the three questions I asked about it, and I have found a big important subject which is a theme in the poem. With a novel or play I would now choose a passage for close discussion, but with a short poem it is possible to look at the whole of the text, and this is what I shall do as I start to explore how it presents the theme of death. Notice that I still only understand a small part of the poem: there are several phrases which are still completely baffling at this stage. For example, I have not yet tried to work out what the poem means by 'curse, bless, me now with your fierce tears', in line 17. On the other hand, I have overcome the problem of being baffled by the whole poem: I now know something about it, that death is a central theme of this poem, and I can use what I know as a way in and expand my understanding as I go on.

2 Analyse the text

Treat the whole poem in the same way as I treated the short passages from *Wuthering Heights*: reread it, looking for points about the theme you are studying. Your aim is to discover how the theme is portrayed in the poem. Death is a big and broad subject: what particular thoughts and feelings about death do we find in this poem? The poet repeats the same two lines about death. 'Do not go gentle into that good night' warns against being calm in the face of death and meekly accepting it as inevitable. 'Rage, rage against the dying of the light' describes the opposite attitude: feelings of helpless fury and pain which rage against death. These two opposite feelings about death, one of which the poet rejects and the other which he encourages, are clearly important because I see they are expressed again and again; so I can feel confident that I have found how death is portrayed in the poem.

You might think that these two points about death, and the poet's feelings about them, jump out at you so obviously that there must be something else hidden behind; but it is worth stressing again that the self-evident answer is often also the best one. I need not worry if the answers are obvious, because I have achieved what I set out to do in Step 2. Now I have moved on from the broad idea of death, and I understand how it is an issue which affects the poet's feelings. The repetitive insistence of his urgings to 'rage' against death shows that these are crucial feelings for him, so I can move on to the next step confident that I understand how the theme is a vital crisis issue in the poem.

3 *Relate the part you have studied to the text as a whole*

In Step 3 you build on what you know, hoping to find out more. You know two things about the poem: the background situation, and how the theme is portrayed. In Step 3 put these two things together. The method to use is the same as for a novel or play: turn what you know into a question which helps you to discover more. This is how to formulate a useful leading question about the poem you are study-ing. First, write a sentence explaining the background situation: 'Dylan Thomas wrote a poem to his dying father about death'. Second, write a sentence explaining the theme you have studied: 'Death is described in terms of two opposite attitudes: calm accep-tance, and raging fury against death'. You want to find out how and why the two things you know fit together in the poem, so you need a question which asks this. In order to understand the purpose, the aim of the poem, ask the question 'Why?' Here is the question I would ask about Dylan Thomas's poem: 'Why does Dylan Thomas write to his dying father telling him to be angry and not calm about death?' As when you study a novel or a play, then, use this technique of turning what you know into a question to help you build up your knowledge and develop your ideas.

When you have rephrased what you know as a question, reread the poem looking for answers. In this case there is a clear and natural answer: Dylan Thomas is deeply upset by his father's approaching death, and the poem expresses his grief and the helpless anger he feels. You will often find that the first answer to your question seems almost too obvious. Again, do not ignore these self-evident points, because they are the most direct link between the poet's feelings and the writing of the poem. The text may be very complex, but the familiar feelings you can understand easily go a long way towards explaining why the poet wrote the poem.

Now I can look more specifically for an answer to my question in terms of the theme of death. What about the two attitudes to death? Why does Thomas write to his father about these? Thomas's feelings are clear. He is firmly committed to rage against death, and he rejects the idea that anybody could be calm about it. In particular he wants his father to rage against death. There is an urgency about the way he repeats his command, suggesting that Thomas could not bear to see his father die calmly; and this impression is heightened by the way he asks his father to 'curse, bless' him with his 'fierce tears', in line 17. This phrase is one of the baffling parts of the poem: how can anything curse and bless at the same time? They are opposites, so your first reaction might be to say, 'It doesn't make sense'. Now, however, you know a lot about the background situation and the theme of death. What seems meaningless at first can often make clear sense at this later stage. Look at 'curse' and 'bless' one by one, and see how they fit into the context of the poem as a whole. How will his father's tears and anger 'curse' the poet? For the same reason which makes Thomas upset: it is painful to see someone you love in misery, in helpless fury, dying. The feelings Thomas is asking for are a 'curse' because they are painful expressions of love shared between father and son. How, then, can his father's rage 'bless' him? It will reassure him that his father shares his own feelings of rage against death. He loves his father and does not want him to die: he wants him to fight for life and hate death. If they feel the same way, this will 'bless' Dylan Thomas. That, at least, is how I understand this difficult line, and it seems to fit in with everything I have discovered about how Thomas presents the theme of death in the poem.

In Step 3, then, you can come back to many parts of the poem which seem baffling at first. Look closely at them, perhaps even word by word, and you will find that the study you have done in the first two steps bears fruit: you will begin to see how these difficult parts fit into the context of the poem as a whole. I have now completed Step 3, and I understand the poem much better than when I read it for the first time. There are still a number of difficult lines I have not tried to explain, so I have not finished studying the poem. However, finding and studying a theme has helped me over the problem of starting to study: as with *Wuthering Heights*, approaching the text through a major theme has opened a door into understanding what the whole work is about. I now have a reliable framework of understanding, a confident idea of what the poem expresses, which I can use as a basis when I come to study other aspects of the text.

'Do Not Go Gentle into That Good Night' gives its message in the title, and repeats it at the end of each stanza. What can you do if the poem you are studying is less direct? In many poems, the main meaning is **implied**, and the surface of the poem gives you little to go on. My next example is a poem of this sort, and I shall show that you can use the same method with confidence to come to grips with more difficult poetry. Be methodical, and do not allow yourself to feel baffled. Focus on what you know and build on that, and the poem's meaning will become clearer and clearer. I have chosen 'The Tyger' by William Blake, a poem so well known that many people can recite the first verse from memory, but few can explain what it means.

'The Tyger' by William Blake

Tyger Tyger, burning bright,
In the forests of the night;
What immortal hand or eye,
Could frame thy fearful symmetry?

In what distant deeps or skies,
Burnt the fire of thine eyes?
On what wings dare he aspire?
What the hand, dare sieze the fire?

And what shoulder, & what art,
Could twist the sinews of thy heart?
And when thy heart began to beat,
What dread hand? & what dread feet?

What the hammer? what the chain,
In what furnace was thy brain?
What the anvil? what dread grasp,
Dare its deadly terrors clasp?

When the stars threw down their spears
And water'd heaven with their tears:
Did he smile his work to see?
Did he who made the Lamb make thee?

Tyger Tyger burning bright,
In the forests of the night:
What immortal hand or eye,
Dare frame thy fearful symmetry?

(from *Songs of Innocence and Experience*, Rupert Hart-Davis, 1967, plate 42)

1 *Think about the text*

You have read the poem, and feel the rousing grandeur of its rhythm
and fine phrases. But what is it about? You hear the four grand
thumps of rhythm in 'Tyger Tyger, burning bright': it is wonderful to
read and listen to, but how does a tiger burn? You read 'fearful symmetry': an impressive phrase, but what does it mean? Think of the
poem as a crisis from an unwritten story, and start by finding out about
the situation, using our three initial questions. **In what circumstances was the poem written?** 'The Tyger' does not tell us where
the poet is or what has happened before the poem. All we know is that,
either in reality or in imagination, the poet is looking at a tiger. **To
whom is the poem addressed?** Blake begins with 'Tyger Tyger'
and says 'thy' symmetry, brain, eyes and so on. The poet talks directly
to the tiger, then. There is another character, called 'he', in the poem.
'He' is the person or being who created the tiger. **What is the main
thing the poem expresses?** The poet asks the tiger a question in the
first and last stanzas, and several other questions in between. The main
question is 'What God could "frame thy fearful symmetry"?' The
phrase about symmetry is still confusing, so I will not dwell on it at this
stage. Is there anything clearer elsewhere? Yes, there is a plainer question: 'Did he who made the Lamb make thee?' So the poet asks the
tiger 'Who created you?' This question is the main thing the poem
expresses. My summary of the situation, then, is as follows: the poet
addresses a tiger and asks 'Who created you?'

I have now pieced together enough to begin looking for a theme.
Is there a big subject, part of everyone's life and thought, that is a
subject of this poem? The poet's questions make one theme obvious:
the theme of creation. Creation is a big subject which is on the poet's
mind. Remember not to ignore the obvious, because any understanding you grasp in Step 1 is enough to build upon. If you have
found a theme, however self-evident it is, move on to the next step. I
have completed Step 1 by saying that creation is a theme of 'The
Tyger'.

2 *Analyse the text*

Creation is a big subject, so you want to find out more detail about the
elements that make up the theme. What, in particular, does the poet
say about the theme? Reread the poem, looking for points about crea-

tion. In 'The Tyger', the poet asks his main question at the beginning and the end, and asks the same question about various parts of the tiger, such as brain, heart and eyes, in between. Only one line, however, reveals more than I already knew. 'Did he who made the Lamb make thee?' contrasts the fierce tiger with a meek lamb. This tells me that the poet is interested in the variety and contrasts in crea-tion. His question can be summarised as: 'how can one being have created two such contrasting creatures as a tiger and a lamb?' Reread-ing has taught me something, then, but not as much as I hoped. This is because the main theme of 'The Tyger' is not expressed in the poem's surface meaning, unlike the main theme of Dylan Thomas's 'Do No Go Gentle into That Good Night'. At this stage I want to discover more but I cannot do so just by reading what the poem says.

What are you looking for at this point? The answer is the parti-cular points, about a big subject, which are on the poet's mind and which move the poet to express his feelings. Remember that literature is about ordinary life, and a poet is not a mysterious and different creature. Imagine you have a friend who is engaged to be married. She is happy, but you notice her moods and say to yourself: 'I wonder what it is about marriage that is preoccupying her?' That would be a natural question to ask, and is exactly the question to use here. Look at the poem as a whole and ask: 'What preoccupies Blake about creation?' Now I can look at the poem again, but in a different way. I am not looking for 'points' about creation or 'what the poet says' about it. Instead I look for signs of a preoccupation, signs of what is on Blake's mind. In the same way, if your friend does not tell you what troubles her, you observe her, listen to the way she talks, and work out what is behind her moods from this.

When I look at Blake's poem in this way, his preoccupations stand out clearly. Terror and fear leap out from the poem: 'fearful', 'dare', 'dare', 'dread', 'dread', 'dread', 'dare', 'deadly terrors', 'dare' and 'fearful'. Blake conveys the fearful power of both the tiger and the creator. Also, I am struck by the tone of his questions. His tone is like astonishment and wonder: 'Can it be? Is it possible?' In fact, the way in which Blake asks 'who made you?' implies the answer. Look at the first question, summarised as a statement to bring out its implication:

Tiger, with your eyes burning brightly in the darkness, you are so perfect and terrifying that I can hardly imagine the infinite power and courage of God, your creator.

This tells me that Blake feels awe at the sheer power of creation; I already knew, from line 20, that he feels amazement at the contrasts in creation. Now I summarise the other questions, in my mind. Most of them express parts of the main question, but one of them tells me something new. Look at my summary of line 19:

> It is hard for me to understand how God could be pleased, and smile with pleasure, after creating such a frightening thing as the tiger.

This goes further than amazement. Here, Blake is concerned because many of God's creations, like the tiger, seem frightful, hostile and destructive: they can often seem evil. Yet God is supposed to be good. 'How can I understand God's purpose in putting so much destructiveness and fear into the world?' is another way of putting Blake's question.

I have now completed Step 2. I looked at the theme of creation in 'The Tyger', and found that Blake is particularly overwhelmed by the power of and contrasts in creation; and that he struggles to understand God's goodness because creation is so frightening and bewildering. I now know a great deal more about how the theme of creation is brought out in the poem, and I am ready to move on to Step 3. Notice that the theme of this poem is more difficult to analyse than was the case with 'Do Not Go Gentle into That Good Night'. I used my method, and built on what I knew; but I had to be flexible. I was helped by thinking about the theme in a different way, looking for 'signs of preoccupation' rather than 'points'; and I rephrased parts of the poem in different ways, re-expressing questions as statements, and summarising. When you approach poems, use the method demonstrated here, but do not be frightened to adapt to the characteristics of the poem you are studying. As you practise, you will develop **flexibility of approach** within the secure framework of the three-step method I have demonstrated.

3 *Relate the part you have studied to the text as a whole*

Begin this step by formulating a leading question: put together what you have learned in Steps 1 and 2, and re-express them as a question which will help to develop your insight into the poem. In Step 1 I learned that the poet wonders about creation when looking at a tiger; and in Step 2 I found that the power and variety of creation, and fear of nature's apparent hostility, make it a struggle for the poet to understand God. Remember that the most effective leading questions start with 'why?' because you want to discover the writer's purpose. I can turn this information into a leading question thus: why does the poet put so much emphasis on power, strength, violence and fear in his poem about creation?

Now reread the poem looking for answers. In 'The Tyger' I find that the tiger itself is used as a base to emphasise the greater power and wonder of God. The tiger is 'burning' and lives 'in the forest of the night'; its eyes have burning 'fires', its heart is made of twisted 'sinews', and its brain was beaten into shape on an 'anvil' after heating in a 'furnace'. This is the emphasis on power, fear and violence I found in Step 2. Its effect is to make the Creator's power too great to be expressed. All the poet can do is vainly ask questions: if the tiger's power is terrifying, even more terrifying must be the power of God who made the tiger. So I have found an answer to my question: Blake emphasises the tiger's power as a way of conveying a sense of the infinite power of God.

So far my answer has focused on the tiger's power. Now I want to think about fear: how does the emphasis on fear relate to the poem as a whole? Fear is our natural response to the tiger. We all fear violent things, and Blake expresses this insistently. The poem as a whole, on the other hand, suggests that our fear is short-sighted. We may be amazed by creation; but perhaps we should not be frightened of it. After all, the same creator made the lamb and 'Did he smile his work to see?' Perhaps the poet is urging his readers to see beyond fear: he urges us not to be frightened, just because something seems violent and hostile to us. The poet certainly implies that fear is produced by our narrow-mindedness.

I could pursue these thoughts in many fruitful ways. For example, I could think about the poem as a warning against prejudice, telling us not to be frightened of things that are hard to understand, that seem alien at first. Or, I could pursue the idea of evil. There is violence and injustice in the world, and I could think about this poem as an attempt to reconcile the world's apparent evil with faith in God. However, I have already gained a great deal from Step 3. This example has demonstrated that our method will work even with a less direct, more 'difficult' poem. The process of finding a start, however obvious, and building my understanding from there, has been as successful with Blake's 'The Tyger' as with Dylan Thomas's 'Do Not Go Gentle into That Good Night'.

CONCLUSION

Use the three steps I have explained in this chapter to find a major theme in the text you are studying. This will give you a general idea of what the text is about which you can use as a framework for further study of its other aspects, such as the characters or the style. You will also be starting to amass evidence which can support the points you make in essays, and which show the examiner that you know the text. In the course of this book I will be showing how to focus on different aspects of the texts you study, how to analyse the characters in novels and plays or the structure of a text, and I will be stressing the importance of focusing on the style in which your text is written. All the different aspects you will study, however, contribute to your understanding of the themes. Even the smallest actions of our lives have a bearing on the big issues and problems which confront us; in just the same way, every aspect of a literary text contributes to expanding and illuminating the meaning of the whole work. In other words, the basic sense of what the text is about, which you gain from pinpointing the major themes, helps you to make sense of every aspect of the text and grows richer and more subtle as you study.

2

Looking at characters

CHARACTERS AND THEMES

WHEN you read a novel or play for the first time, you are likely to be struck by the story, and also by the characters. The characters are the people in a text, they are part of the ordinary life that you meet as you read. You might dislike, admire or sympathise with them, but whatever they do or say or feel they account for a large part of your first unstudied response. I shall therefore use characters as our next starting-point in studying literature.

Initially all you will have is just a general idea of what the characters are like. As with themes, however, we want to go beyond this first impression and explore the characters in detail. In this chapter I shall show how to use the same three logical steps we used in Chapter 1 to think about the character you are studying, to analyse a selected crisis in detail, and finally to relate what you have learned about your character to the text as a whole. We can use the same steps because your aim in studying a character is the same as when approaching themes: you want to develop a close, detailed understanding of the text and then see how the complex details fit into and enrich your broad grasp of the whole text.

How does a character fit into a text as a whole? Many students find this point difficult to grasp because each character has a different relationship with the other characters and so there is a . multiplicity of detailed observations you can make about the text. The key to solving this problem is simply to remind yourself that characters are the people who live and experience the themes, and so finding a major theme which is important in your character's life will help you relate the person you are studying to the big issues of the world in which they exist. Of course, you want to know about the character in detail, but to gain that all-important grasp of how they fit into the text as a whole, focus on their involvement with a major theme and this will provide the broad framework you need for developing your ideas.

Generally, characters in both novels and plays can be approached in the same way. The main section of this chapter shows in detail how you can use the three steps to study a character in a novel, while the final section explains how the same approach can be applied to plays, and also gives some extra hints to help you study characters from drama.

Elizabeth Bennet, from *Pride and Prejudice* by Jane Austen

You have been asked, or have decided, to look at the character of Elizabeth Bennet. Adopting the three-step approach illustrated in Chapter 1, you begin with some thoughts on the text as a whole, seeking to clarify and organise your first unstudied response to the novel.

1 *Think about the text*

When you have read the text, you know two things about a character: you know what they are like and their story, the part of their life that is told you in the story of the text. As with themes, begin by using what you know at the start. In this step I shall explain how to think about the kind of person you are studying to find a major theme which is important in their life; and how to think about their story to pinpoint the crises they go through. When you have done these two things, the initial thinking step will be over: you will have found a crisis ready to look at in detail in Step 2, and you will have a major theme in mind which will help you relate the character to the world of the text as you study. First, however, we have to go through Step 1.

You know what the character is like. This impression of a person is made up of a lot of details you picked up in reading: what they look like, how they speak and dress, their social class, interests and opinions, and suchlike. The first thing to do is write a brief description using these details, concentrating on what they are like and what is important in their life. Your aim is to reveal the kind of personality you are dealing with, so you can link him or her with one of the major themes of the text, as I shall be doing with Jane Austen's Elizabeth Bennet.

Before I describe Elizabeth Bennet, however, here are some general hints which will help you with any text. First, the character's name will often indicate what sort of person they are. For example, Heathcliff in *Wuthering Heights* proves to be as wild and rugged as his name suggests. Secondly, there is often a description of the character when they are first introduced, which will give you a lot of information about what they look like and wear, and at the same time begin to reveal their personality. Finally, there are usually a lot of conversations about anyone new who has just been introduced. This is natural: people talk about someone they have just met. Remind yourself of the conversations near to where your character is introduced and find out what others think about the person you are studying. These are hints on how to make your description thorough and revealing; but your main concern, as I have said, is to work out what is important about them and what issues are crucial in their life. Here is my description of Elizabeth Bennet. I have called upon my memory of the text, helped by dipping into the opening chapters to check some of the details.

Elizabeth Bennet is the second of five daughters in the Bennet family. They live on their family estate, Longbourn, and are well-off. However, because they are all girls the estate will pass to a male cousin, and so Elizabeth has no great fortune to make her an attractive catch in the marriage market. She is, though, clever and witty, and has more frank and daring opinions than other people around her. The author does not describe Elizabeth, but the eager Mr Bingley thinks her 'very pretty' (*Pride and Prejudice*, Penguin, 1972, p. 59), while the critical Mr Darcy calls her 'tolerable, but not handsome enough to tempt me' (p. 59), until he notices her 'fine eyes' (p. 73) which he finds very attractive. The time is the end of the eighteenth century, and Elizabeth is twenty years old.

When you have written a description like this, think about it and work out what is important in your character's life. You want to find a subject which is a major theme in the text, and which is a vital issue or problem affecting the life of the character you are studying. Think about my description of Elizabeth. What is the biggest problem she faces in life? The answer is marriage. Her father's death would make her poor, and in the eighteenth century the only way a woman of Elizabeth's class could be comfortable and respectable was through marriage. So the problem of finding a man in her own social class whom she can love and who loves her is the vital problem Elizabeth faces as a young woman. A moment's thought about *Pride and Prejudice* tells me that marriage is also a major theme in the novel as a whole, and so I have found an issue which connects Elizabeth with the world of the text.

Having established these links between character and theme in the novel I can now turn to Elizabeth's story, and identify a crisis to study in detail in the next step. Look for events which bring about a change in the character you are studying: this will help you to identify the crucial experiences in their life, because crises change people, giving them new ideas and new feelings. Here is the story of Elizabeth Bennet. Thinking about the changes in her character has helped me to identify two places where she seems to go through crucial or 'crisis' experiences, and I will pinpoint these places as we come to them.

At the beginning of the novel Elizabeth meets Mr Bingley, his rich friend Mr Darcy, the penniless but handsome officer Mr Wickham, and her cousin the reverend Mr Collins. Elizabeth likes Bingley, who falls in love with her elder sister, Jane. She is repelled by the haughty manners of Darcy, although he is handsome and rich. She likes Wickham and believes him when he slanders Darcy. Collins proposes to Elizabeth, but she rejects him. Bingley and Darcy leave the area suddenly, and Elizabeth is upset: she blames Darcy for separating Bingley and Jane. Elizabeth visits her friend Charlotte who is now Mrs Collins. She meets Darcy again and he proposes to her, but she rejects him, angrily explaining that she hates him for his cruelty to Wickham and to Jane. Darcy sends her a letter which reveals that Wickham is a villain, and shows he had no intention of hurting Jane. On reading Darcy's letter, Elizabeth realises how wrong she has been and feels ashamed. She changes her opinions of Wickham and Darcy. Thinking about Elizabeth's story, I can stop at this point because she has changed: she realises that she has been wrong, and completely changes her mind about Darcy and Wickham. Something about Darcy's proposal and his subsequent letter, then, provokes a crisis in Elizabeth's life.

When Elizabeth returns home, Wickham and the regiment leave for Brighton and her sister Lydia goes with them as a guest of the colonel's wife. Soon after, Elizabeth goes on holiday and happens to visit Darcy's fine home, where she meets him again by chance. He is all kindness and Elizabeth begins to like him. However, the news that Lydia has eloped with Wickham interrupts her holiday and she rushes home. When Elizabeth hears of the elopement, a family disgrace which puts marriage with Darcy beyond her reach, she suddenly realises that she is in love with him. I can stop here again: Elizabeth's feelings have changed. The news of Lydia's elopement precipitates another crisis in Elizabeth's life. The rest of the story tells how Darcy arranges a respectable marriage between the runaways, and finally, after some further anxieties, proposes again to Elizabeth, who accepts him this time. Bingley and Jane also come together, so the novel ends with two happy marriages.

As I thought about Elizabeth's part in the story, I found two crises in her life: first, when she realises that she has been completely wrong about Darcy, and second when she realises that she is in love with him. It would be rewarding to study both these episodes in detail, but to save space I am going to choose just the first of them to look at in detail in Step 2.

Step 1 is now complete. I have found a major theme which is a crucial issue in Elizabeth's life, and I have identified a crisis when she is deeply involved and her character changes. You should be able to see that this step in studying a character is very much the same as the first step in studying a theme. This time you are thinking about one character rather than about the whole text, but you need to think positively, and make vital decisions about what to focus on and where to look in detail, in exactly the same way.

2 Analyse the text

Begin by rereading the crisis episode. This is the step that brings you very close to the text and makes you study in detail; the purpose is to make your ideas precise by close analysis, so that you find the complexity in what you are studying. When you are studying a character, you can have a clear idea of what you are looking for as you reread the crisis. This is because you already know some of the major points about your character's thoughts and feelings. I know that Elizabeth 'hates' Darcy at the beginning of *Pride and Prejudice*, and 'loves' him at the end, and I know that the subject of marriage is important to her. In this step I want to find out about the specific elements that make up Elizabeth, and the precise ways in which the vital issues she is facing affect her, and I hope to develop a complex understanding of Elizabeth in her world from looking closely at the crisis episode.

At this point, however, I am still faced with too much text to study in detail, so I have to narrow the focus again, selecting short passages to analyse closely. This is the same process of logical selection that I illustrated in Chapter 1, but with characters you can find the crucial short passages in a different way. Characters reveal their complex feelings when they do or say something puzzling, illogical or inconsistent. As you reread the crisis, then, look for any passages which show your character acting or speaking in a puzzling or contradictory way. If anything about your character does not match something else in their personality, or if they behave in an odd or inexplicable way, make a note of the passage which shows this. This will be a crucial passage to look at in closer detail.

I am going to analyse Chapter 34 of *Pride and Prejudice*, when Darcy proposes to Elizabeth. It will help if I give an outline first. At the beginning of the chapter Elizabeth is alone, rereading her sister Jane's letters and brooding on Darcy's cruelty. She is interrupted by the arrival of Darcy, who declares his love for her and asks her to marry him. At first she feels flattered by his love and sorry for him, but when she notices that he expects her to say yes, she becomes angry. She rejects him, telling him that she has always hated him and she cannot even feel sorry for him. He asks why she hates him, and she explains that it is on account of Wickham and Jane. Darcy apologises for proposing and leaves quickly. As soon as he is gone, Elizabeth breaks down and cries for half an hour. She rushes away when Mr and Mrs Collins return because she is in no state to face them.

When you reread, pick out anything about your character which does not match up. As I look at this chapter, I can see two points about Elizabeth which are rather puzzling. First, she feels complimented by Darcy's love, and is sorry for him, but then she says that she cannot feel any pity for him at all. Is Elizabeth, for some reason, not telling Darcy the truth about her feelings? I shall look closely at this short passage to find out exactly how her complex feelings and behaviour work. Second, when Darcy leaves, Elizabeth sits down and cries for half and hour. This is puzzling because it does not match other parts of the novel. Mr Collins proposed to Elizabeth, and he was much more of a nuisance than Darcy because he would not take no for an answer. Elizabeth was amused, not upset. Why does she break down and cry now? I want to look at this passage more closely, then, to find out about the complex feelings that make her break down in tears.

The method I have used here is like the approach to themes in Chapter 1: it involves rereading the crisis episode, then selecting passages short enough to study in detail. Once I have done this I am ready to look at the complexity of the character I am studying, and I am confident that I will find out about Elizabeth because I have logically selected passages which are crucial to her character. Here is the first of the two passages I want to examine:

> In spite of her deeply-rooted dislike, she could not be insensible to the compliment of such a man's affection, and though her intentions did not vary for an instant, she was at first sorry for the pain he was to receive; till, roused to resentment by his subsequent language, she lost all compassion in anger. She tried, however, to compose herself to answer him with patience, when he should have done. He concluded with representing to her the strength of that attachment which, in spite of all his endeavours, he had found impossible to conquer; and with expressing his hope that it would now be rewarded by her acceptance of his hand. As he said this, she could easily see that he had no doubt of a favourable answer. He *spoke* of apprehension and anxiety, but his countenance expressed real security. Such a circumstance could only exasperate farther, and, when he ceased, the colour rose into her cheeks, and she said –
> 'In such cases as this, it is, I believe, the established mode to express a sense of obligation for the sentiments avowed, however unequally they may be returned. It is natural that obligation should be felt, and if I could *feel* gratitude, I would now thank you. But I cannot – I have never desired your good opinion, and you have certainly bestowed it most unwillingly'.
>
> (p. 221)

I have chosen this passage, remember, because Elizabeth appears contradictory in her behaviour to Darcy. She 'could not be insensible to the compliment of such a man's affection' and she was 'sorry for the pain he was to receive'; yet she tells him categorically that she 'cannot' feel any gratitude for him and she has 'never' desired his good opinion. Her real feelings, then, are a complex mixture of gratitude and sympathy, but she only shows Darcy a simple feeling of hatred. When you spot an inconsistency in your character, look closely at the passage to find out why it happens: what is it in their thoughts and feelings that makes them contradict themselves? In the case of the passage I am looking at, why does Elizabeth pretend to hate Darcy more than she actually does? The passage explains how it happens: Darcy makes her angry by showing that he expects her to say yes, and by telling her that the social gulf between them made him unwilling to fall in love with her. She was 'roused to resentment', she 'lost all compassion in anger' and his confidence could only 'exasperate farther'. Elizabeth lashes out with her pretence of hatred because his confidence makes her angry: she rebels against what he expects her to do.

Characters are always involved in their world, and so it is worthwhile considering what an ordinary person would have done in the same situation. In Elizabeth's case, a little thought gives me the answer: most young women in her place would have seized the chance of marrying Darcy, because he is rich and from an aristocratic family. Darcy expects Elizabeth to accept him, and so would almost everyone else. This also makes Elizabeth angry; it is clear that by reacting against Darcy, she is also rebelling against the conventions of her society.

From analysing this short passage closely, then, I have learned that Elizabeth's feelings about Darcy are more complex than she will admit; and that society's cynical values also play a part in making her angry. Here is the second passage I chose to analyse, when Elizabeth breaks down in tears:

> The tumult of her mind was now painfully great. She knew not how to support herself, and from actual weakness sat down and cried for half-an-hour. Her astonishment, as she reflected on what had passed, was increased by every review of it. That she should receive an offer of marriage from Mr Darcy! that he should have been in love with her for so many months! so much in love as to wish to marry her in spite of all the objections which had made him prevent his friend's marrying her sister, and which must appear at least with equal force in his own case – was almost incredible! – it was gratifying to have inspired unconsciously so strong an affection. But his pride, his abominable pride – his shameless avowal of what he had done with respect to Jane – his unpardonable assurance in acknowledging, though he could not justify it, and the unfeeling manner in which he had mentioned Mr Wickham, his cruelty towards whom he had not attempted to deny, soon overcame the pity which the consideration of his attachment had for a moment excited.
>
> (pp. 224-5)

This passage explains more about the complexity of Elizabeth's feelings. I am seeking the same kind of answer as before: why does she sit and cry for half an hour? The passages tell me the answer. Her mind is in 'tumult' which is 'painfully great'. The tumult is because her feelings are in conflict with each other. She is flattered because Darcy loves her, and admires the strength of his love which has overcome the social barriers between them. These feelings lead her to 'pity' him. On the other hand, his pride and his apparent cruelty towards Jane and Wickham turn her against him: these thoughts 'soon overcame' her other feelings. Elizabeth's distress in this passage intensifies my impression of the conflicting feelings I found in the first passage: her feelings for Darcy are a mixture of sympathy and abhorrence, and this passage tells me that these emotions must be very strong, because the battle between them makes her break down and cry.

I can also look in this passage for clues to Elizabeth's reaction to the issue of marriage. I know from the passage that she rebelled against Darcy's and the world's expectation that she would marry him for his money and position. In this passage her 'pity' is excited, and she is 'gratified' and feels astonishment because Darcy's love has overcome the social barriers between them. I can now see that Elizabeth's feelings about marriage and social position are in tumult as well. She is flattered by Darcy's social superiority, but also hostile to it.

From my two passages I have learned a lot about Elizabeth's complex feelings. When you reach this point it is helpful to remind yourself that the reason why you selected the crisis in the first place was because the character you are studying changes or develops. I know that Elizabeth changes her opinion of Darcy and Wickham after this crisis; and I know that the 'tumult' she is experiencing is made up of conflicting feelings about Darcy and the issue of marriage. These two aspects of my understanding are still rather separate, however, so I want to find out more about the dynamics of the character I am working on: I want to find out how the crisis works and how she changes. To do this, put the crisis into context. Simply think about the complexities you have discovered, and see them as part of the character's broader 'story'. When you have thought about how the crisis works and how the character changes, you will be able to confirm your ideas and define their change by focusing again, this time choosing a short passage which describes the character after the crisis episode. Your aim is to gain a well-defined understanding of exactly what has happened to the individual character you are studying.

Let us return to Elizabeth Bennet: how does she change? A little thought about the build-up to this crisis helps me to grasp what happens to her: she hated Darcy, and she was revolted by the idea of marrying for money. When he proposed, he inspired new feelings and ideas which Elizabeth had not expected: she pitied him and felt gratitude, and she had never expected a rich man to offer her his love. She was ready for love or money, but could not cope with both together. Obviously this new situation meant that she was forced to alter her feelings and ideas. How did she alter them?

The different characters you study will respond to crises in a variety of different ways: their changes might be subtle and difficult to pin down. Be open-minded, therefore. Reread the text, looking carefully at what happens until the crisis events are over, then simply choose a passage which describes the character you are studying. This method will work: however slight or unexpected your character's reaction to the crisis may be, you will find out just how much or how little it has affected them.

I now need, then, to reread the rest of Elizabeth's crisis episode. Chapter 35 is taken up with Darcy's letter. In Chapter 36 I find Elizabeth's reaction to the letter: how she reads it angrily once, and decides not to read it again, then reads it a second time forcing herself to be fair, and realises that Darcy was right and she was wrong all along. The passage I am looking for comes soon after her second reading of the letter, when she realises how wrong she has been:

> She grew absolutely ashamed of herself. Of neither Darcy nor Wickham could she think without feeling that she had been blind, partial, prejudiced, absurd.
>   'How despicably have I acted!' she cried; 'I, who have prided myself on my discernment! I, who have valued myself on my abilities! who have often disdained the generous candour of my sister, and gratified my vanity in useless or blameable distrust. How humiliating is this discovery! yet, how just a humiliation! Had I been in love, I could not have been more wretchedly blind. But vanity, not love, has been my folly. Pleased with the preference of one, and offended by the neglect of the other, on the very beginning of our acquaintance, I have courted prepossession and ignorance, and driven reason away, where either was concerned. Till this moment I never knew myself.'
>
> (pp. 236-7)

This passage explains how the crisis has changed Elizabeth. She was proud of being clever, and vain about being more perceptive than other people. This led her to do the opposite of what society expected. In this passage she realises that her vanity has been her undoing: she was flattered because Wickham paid attention to her, and took against Darcy for ignoring her. The crisis has changed Elizabeth, then, by 'humiliating' her: she now feels that she is not specially clever but just as vain as any young girl who wants to be flattered by handsome men. After the crisis her opinions of Wickham and Darcy are reversed, as I already knew from looking at her story in Step 1. Now, however, I can appreciate the depth of the change that has taken place in her character: after the crisis she is less conceited about her cleverness. Being humiliated has taught her to be more careful in making judgements, and to look more critically at her own feelings and motives.

I now have quite a full understanding of this crisis. I have found out a good deal about Elizabeth's feelings and her ideas about marriage, and I have a clear sense of how her character works, of how she changes under stress. In addition, I can see how the major theme of marriage is a complex issue for her, and that its complexity is involved in the crisis which brings about a change in her personality.

When you study characters like this, you will often find that you discover things about their feelings that they do not know themselves. You should never guess about a character, however. Base all your conclusions on close analysis of the vital short passages you focus on. Although Elizabeth did not understand her own mistakes until afterwards, Jane Austen clearly did understand her complexity. An author conveys complexity by portraying the character's behaviour, and the method I have shown helps you to understand what the author conveys, whether the character knows about it or not.

3 Relate the part you have studied to the text as a whole

The character you are studying is a complex person who seems almost alive, and certainly your close work in Step 2 should increase your sense of the felt life of the character. In your third step, however, you need to gain a broad view of the text again because you want to find out how a person's life and experiences can contribute to the meaningful imagined world of the whole text, how a character is part of what the text is about. As usual at the beginning of this third step, look for the right sort of leading question to develop your ideas. You want to relate your character to a major theme. In Step 1, you found an issue in the text which is important to your character; in Step 2, you studied your character in crisis as he or she confronts this issue; now you are going to concentrate on the specific aspects of the theme that relate directly to your character.

In Step 1, then, I found that marriage is a major theme that affects Elizabeth. Now I understand that marriage is a complex issue for her because she is faced with the conflict between society's view, that young women should marry for money, and her own feeling that marriage should be about love. I found that Elizabeth gives a confused reacton to this problem: she searches for love but seems over-angry about the need for money in marriage. Now I can broaden my view of her character, building on what I found out from one crisis, and ask:

how do Elizabeth's experiences in the novel as a whole relate to its concern with money and love in marriage?

There are two particular ways in which characters and themes relate to each other and which help us to see what we are looking for in the text at this stage. First, **Characters contribute to the themes** when they think and talk about the subjects important in their lives. Second, situations arise where the character's life is affected by the major themes of the text, so you can say that **characters experience the themes**. Using these two ideas you can think about your character positively, and develop an understanding of the complex involvement between character and theme. Here is a short discussion of Elizabeth Bennet and the theme of marriage in *Pride and Prejudice*.

First, what does Elizabeth think or say about marriage, how does she contribute to this theme? All we have to do is find where she gives an opinion on this theme. The quickest way to do this and to gain an overall sense of how a character's ideas on the theme develop is to take an example from near the beginning of the text and another one from near the end. This gives you an idea of how much their ideas develop, and your work on a crisis in Step 2 helps you to see how these changes came about.

Elizabeth talks about marriage with her friend Charlotte near the beginning of *Pride and Prejudice*. Charlotte says that the most important thing is to catch a well-off man, and the couple can get to know each other after the wedding. Elizabeth is shocked at Charlotte's cynicism. She says: 'You make me laugh, Charlotte; but it is not sound. You know it is not sound, and that you would never act in this way yourself' (p. 70). I know that the theme of marriage focuses on the problem of reconciling the conflict between love and money. This detail from the beginning of the novel tells me that Elizabeth does not accept society's commercial ideas: she believes in love. At the beginning of the novel, then, Elizabeth contributes her romantic idealism to the theme of marriage.

In the crisis I analysed, I saw how the simple choice between love and money becomes a complex real situation when Darcy offers both, and Elizabeth finds herself torn by conflicting impulses: admiration of his love, but resentment of his money and social rank. Near the end of the novel, however, Elizabeth quarrels with Darcy's aunt, who comes to dissuade her from marrying above herself. Their quarrel leads Elizabeth to express her feelings about marriage and love, and the social differences between herself and Darcy. First, she insists that she has the right to choose her husband without respect to society's views: 'I am only resolved to act in that manner which will, in my own opinion, constitute my happiness' (p. 367). In the same quarrel Elizabeth also asserts that in spite of the petty social differences between them, she now feels that she is Darcy's equal: 'He is a gentleman; I am a gentleman's daughter: so far we are equal' (p. 366). Elizabeth's contributions to the theme of marriage at the end of the novel, then, show that she has developed. At the beginning of the novel she had a simple, romantic view of marriage and could not cope with the complexity of real-life decisions, where financial and emotional considerations were entangled together. Now, however, she confidently makes a complicated decision and dismisses the petty social and financial barriers which previously upset her. At the same time, notice that she still believes in love, as she insists on her right to marry for 'happiness'.

You can find further contributions your character makes to the theme in other parts of the text, enriching your understanding of how their attitude changes. Elizabeth's ideas about marriage become more complex and balanced through her experiences in the story, and what she learns makes a major contribution to the way this theme develops through the novel. Study what your character says about the theme, then, and you will see how their ideas and feelings contribute to the complex development of themes in the text as a whole.

Now I can turn to how Elizabeth *experiences* the theme: how do the issues associated with marriage affect her life? The prospect of marriage comes up repeatedly in what happens to her: she receives three proposals, feels tempted to marry Wickham, and sees her friend and two of her sisters choose husbands. These experiences bring the issue of marriage into the forefront of her life, particularly in the form of choices about love and money, which I can look at quite systematically, as follows. Elizabeth receives offers from one rich man (Darcy), one well-off man from her own class (Collins), and she is tempted to fall in love with a poor man (Wickham). So she directly faces the full range of choices in terms of money. She also indirectly experiences both of the would-have-been situations that she turns down, because Mr Collins marries her friend Charlotte, and Mr Wickham marries her sister Lydia. Elizabeth sees that Charlotte suffers but copes bravely with a husband she cannot love, and Lydia lives an unhappy, insecure life, eventually leading to degradation. Finally, of course, Elizabeth finds love and money combined in her own happy marriage to Darcy.

Notice how thoroughly Jane Austen has constructed the story to give her heroine full and varied experience of this dominant theme.

By this stage you have a good working grasp of the character you are studying as part of the overall pattern and meaning of the text. It is important to see that this is the aim of studying a character: too many students write about characters just as isolated individuals. When you come to write in examinations, the examiner wants you to show that you see how characters are created by the author and make part of the text's meaning and purpose. The approach I have illustrated here keeps this aim firmly in mind, and should ensure that you steadily develop a sense of the complex, two-way relationship between the big issues of the text on the one hand, and the feelings and thoughts of one individual character on the other.

STUDYING CHARACTERS FROM PLAYS

When studying characters in a play you do not have so much on paper to help you: the author does not describe thoughts and feelings or make comments about the characters. On the other hand, by being responsive when you go to the theatre, or by reading imaginatively so that you visualise the drama and 'hear' the lines, you can let the immediacy of dramatic texts help you in understanding what the writer wants to convey. This does not mean that you should approach drama in a different way, but there are two particular hints I shall add to our method that will help you to get the most out of drama. Begin by thinking about how a play works: you hear what people say to each other, and you see them doing things. Events happen in front of your eyes, and the people on stage act out their reactions dramatically. When something terrible happens, the characters' feelings are shown in action: you see the tears and hear the sobs. This explains the supreme importance of dialogue and action in a play, and leads to the two hints I mention now.

In a play, the contradictions in characters are revealed dramatically through contradictory speech and actions. For example, in Shakespeare's *Hamlet* you would notice that Hamlet promises to kill his father's murderer, and he promises to be hard-hearted, not allowing anything to divert him from his revenge. If you are studying Hamlet's character, you can measure his promise against what he does. Watch the stage: what does Hamlet do? He pretends to be mad, shouts at the woman he loves, insults her father, puts on a play, talks about killing himself, and decides not to kill his father's murderer when he has him at his mercy. This is a very brief summary of part of *Hamlet*, but it shows clearly enough that Hamlet says one thing and does another. When you study, look for these differences between speech and action, and ask: why are his actions different from what he says? What complex feelings and thoughts are revealed by this contradiction in the character? Hamlet's failure to carry out the revenge he has sworn reveals a knot of doubts and conflicts in him: his feelings about death, punishment, his enemy and his mother, are all in turmoil. All these work to delay him and divert him from his promised revenge. If you studied Hamlet's character, then, noticing that his speech and actions contradict each other would lead you directly into understanding what complex emotions are at work in him.

The second hint which will help you with characters in plays is to compare them with each other. Again this technique can be applied equally well when you are studying a novel, but I mention it now because comparison and contrast are major ways in which playwrights reveal what a character is like. Think about the other characters in the text, look for people who are in parallel situations with the one you are studying. You can do this in Step 1 when you write a short summary of your character's situation: simply think about the text and ask yourself if any other character is in the same situation. Suppose, again, that I am studying Hamlet. Here is a brief summary of his situation: Hamlet is a young man whose father has been murdered. Is there another young man whose father is murdered? Yes: Laertes' father is killed during the play. Now I have found two characters who are in the same situation, faced by the same issues of grief and revenge. The next thing to do is compare how they respond to their fathers' murders. When Hamlet discovers that his father was murdered, he feigns madness and sets an elaborate trap to make sure that the murderer is really guilty. In other words, Harlet is uncertain and his response to the situation is slow and circuitous. When Laertes learns of this father's death, he draws his sword and rushes fighting his way into the castle, shouting about revenge and ready to kill anyone who gets in his way; so Laertes' reaction is open, direct, and shows no sign of uncertainty. The difference between the two characters reveals how much more doubt and insecurity there is in Hamlet than in the rather simple, forthright personality of Laertes.

I have given only brief descriptions of the situation in *Hamlet*, but they illustrate clearly enough that you can discover the complexity of a character in a play by comparing speech and action, and by comparing your character with someone else who is in the same situation. You will find these methods fruitful because they use the play's immediacy as a help in finding and understanding what the author wants to convey. The overall aim is the same, however, whether you study a novel or a play, because the characters in both are complex people whose feelings and experiences bring to life the big, dominant issues of the text.

CONCLUSION

In these first two chapters I have dealt with the two main approaches to studying a text: most of the work you will do will involve looking at characters and themes. The crucial point to grasp from the method I have illustrated, however, is the kind of understanding you want to arrive at in the end. This should be both precise and broad at the same time. Our three-step method leads you to look closely at short passages, but it also helps you develop an overall sense of what the text is about. It is this grasp of how the rich details, in particular crisis passages, are part of the broad sweep of meaning of the text as a whole that you should aim for when you are working on a text. As you look at a crisis episode try to see how its details bring both character and themes to life, but also how it reflects the overall meaning of the text. What will help you in this, however, is if you have a sense of the shape or form of the text you are studying so that you can see how the crisis you are looking at is part of a larger pattern and is a focal point in the text. This is what I shall be discussing in the next chapter, which looks at the structure, or overall shape, of a literary text.

3

Structure

WHAT IS STRUCTURE?

STRUCTURE is shape. Writers give shape to the texts they produce by fitting characters, places and events into a story which is satisfying and complete. Life itself has no shape: it does not focus on important subjects, but is bitty, cluttered and messy. We could not read about real life because it is so cluttered up and never gets anywhere definite. A literary text, on the other hand, has to be satisfying, complete in itself, and have a clear strong shape. So the author creates an imagined world which has a beginning and an end; important crises bring about important changes, making people and ideas develop. In literature, problems are resolved and a conclusion, an 'end', is reached.

The structure of a text does not do anything or feel anything, unlike characters and themes; it is simply a big framework on which all the text's details hang, holding them together in a big shape. It follows that we hardly notice the structure when we are reading: we are caught up in the characters' lives and the excitement of what happens. Looking at the structure is a different way of looking at the text, then: keep yourself more at a distance from the details, and look for big outstanding points instead. Analysing the structure of a text is a vital part of study, however, because it further develops your sense of how complex details fit into a shaped whole, and so tells you more about the meaning and purpose of the work.

When you study poetry you may often find that themes and subject-matter are not clear at first, that the images and words are so difficult that you cannot pinpoint what it is about. When this happens it is a good idea to look at the poem's structure. A poem is a pattern of words, so you can often see its shape easily even when its meaning is still a puzzle, and this can provide a way to discover what it is about. I will turn to the structure of poems, however, in the second half of this chapter. I start with the structure of novels and plays, showing that all such texts have a lot in common because they share a basic structural pattern.

BASIC STRUCTURE IN NOVELS AND PLAYS

To find the structure, begin by dividing your text into three big sections. I have said that authors create an imagined world with a beginning and an end. These are the first and last big sections to find; but what about the middle? Here, the idea of a crisis helps again. I have shown how you can gain understanding of characters and themes by looking at their stories as a series of crises. Structure works in the same way, but you look at everything on a much larger scale. There are usually several crises in a novel or play, and you can choose to look at any of them to find out about themes and characters. Now, however, look for something bigger: a crisis which is not just one of several, but is the main crisis of the whole text. You can recognise it simply because it makes the story end: the main crisis is drastic and final, and resolves the complications of the whole text, bringing everything to a conclusion.

Now you know the three sections to look for: there is a beginning which introduces the world of the text; a middle section that explores all the problems and complications which build up and make a drastic main crisis happen; and an ending after the main crisis, when the complications have been resolved and a concluding state of affairs is worked out. We can call these sections **exposition, complication** and **resolution**. Here is a more detailed description of them, which will help you to recognise where they are in the texts you study.

In the **exposition** the reader or audience meets the characters, and any past events which help us to understand the situation are explained. In this opening section the author also brings out dominant ideas or aspects of character, announcing the themes of the text. Usually the opening section is bare of action: the reader is getting to know the characters and the situation, so the text often opens during a stable pause before much action can begin. Here you will often find long speeches which explain what happened before the story started, or the characters discussing important themes before the action begins.

As soon as we know enough about the situation and characters, the writer introduces the **complication**: problems or mysteries which will have to be solved, tests for the characters, action and movement. In this section the writer makes the plot happen. The complications of the plot explore the complex nature of the characters and the big issues of the text, and put themes and characters under pressure to force them to an outcome.

In the **resolution**, something drastic finally happens, something which solves problems and mysteries, and either happily or disastrously clears up the complications of the plot. In this last section you can expect the characters to die, marry, or come to terms with their fate: the villain is revealed, the falsely accused is set free, the foundling discovers his parents, the new king is crowned or the tragic hero dies. In the resolution section, then, you find decisive events which dominate and shape the future, just as the writer explains the past in the exposition section at the beginning; the author adds shape to his story by bringing the past and future into the first and last sections of the text.

This simple three-part structure is in evidence in all novels and plays. When you want to look at the structure of a text, start by looking for the main crisis which brings about the ending, which you will find towards the end of the work. When you have found the main crisis you can use it to work out where the three sections are in the text you are studying. Normally we look at structure after looking at some themes and characters as a way of grasping the overall shape behind detailed complexities. I will show how you can do this, using Shakespeare's *Othello* to demonstrate how you can find the structure and what you can learn about a text from seeing its overall shape.

Othello by William Shakespeare

1 Think about the text

Begin in the same way as I have shown in the first two chapters: use the story you know from first reading to help you in making a start. This time, however, think about the story as a whole, as if you are keeping some distance away from it and looking at it as a complete thing without details. You want to find the main crisis, which is usually near the end of the text: the biggest, most important and decisive event of the whole story, which makes the ending happen. Here is an outline of *Othello*. I have kept at a distance from the details of the play, so this is the barest outline of the story.

Othello is a successful Venetian general. The Turks are about to attack Cyprus, and Othello is sent there to take command and defend the island. Before leaving Venice Othello marries Desdemona, daughter of a nobleman. Her father objects because Othello is black, but the Duke overrules him and allows the marriage, and the couple sail for Cyprus. One of Othello's officers is Iago, a resentful and ambitious villain. By various plots he convinces Othello that Desdemona is unfaithful, and Othello murders her. Iago's treachery is then revealed, Othello realises his mistake, and kills himself.

The play begins with Othello's marriage to Desdemona, and most of the action concerns Iago plotting to make him jealous. The big event which makes the tragic ending happen is when Othello kills Desdemona. It is a sudden catastrophic action which brings out the truth and ends the struggle between jealousy and love in Othello. The murder of Desdemona, then, is the main crisis of the play. As I have explained, the main crisis is like a joint or hinge between the second and third sections of the text because it resolves the complications and makes the ending happen. So, before Othello kills his wife is the **complication** section; after this murder, the rest of the play is **resolution**.

Now I want to find the first section: **exposition**. You will often find there is no outstanding event which ends exposition and ushers in complication. There is often a gradual change, or the author moves quickly into the complications while we are still getting to know the characters and learning things about the situation. The most important point, however, is to grasp what exposition does: it introduces you to the people and the world of the text, and brings you up to date with the past. To find and define exposition, then, simply look for a place in the text where you can say these things have been done: you have met the main characters, you know what is happening, and you have an idea of the major issues in the text. Then you can say that exposition is over. Find this place in the text by glancing through the opening scenes or chapters and noting when the main characters come in, and what the text describes and explains. Studying structure means looking for the big units of a text, not the details, so there is no need to reread the opening in detail. All you need to do is have a clear idea of when the different elements of the author's world first appear. Here is a broad idea of the opening scenes of *Othello*.

Act I, scene i introduces Roderigo and Iago, who talk about Othello, and tell Desdemona's father that Othello has stolen his daughter. In scene ii we meet Othello, Iago again and Cassio, and

Desdemona's father rushes in wanting to fight. However, they are all called to the Duke. Scene iii takes place in the Duke's council chamber, and Desdemona appears. The political situation is explained, and Othello is made Governor of Cyprus. We hear about Othello's career, and the story of Othello's and Desdemona's courtship; her father's objections are heard and the Duke gives his judgement in favour of the lovers. At the end of the scene Iago and Roderigo discuss further plots against Othello which they intend to carry out when they get to Cyprus. In the first act, then, all the major characters have appeared, the political and military situation and Othello's courtship have been explained, and Iago's villainy is clear. Exposition is therefore over at the end of the first act.

Step 1 is almost complete, because I have found the three main sections of the text. It is important to remember at this stage that you are making big generalisations about the text. When I say that Act I is exposition, it does not mean there are no complications in Act I. It is useful for us to divide the text into three big sections, because we find it convenient to discuss structure in this way. However, the most important point to grasp is how the story works and what the sections do. When you understand what exposition and complication do, you can see how the play moves gradually from one to the other towards the end of the first act, and how the reality of the text is more complex than the sharp divisions between sections that we use for convenience.

The point of Step 1 is to grasp the three big sections in the text. This puts you in a better position to see the overall development of the work, its characters and themes. You are better placed to understand just how things are different at the end from at the beginning; this helps you to see how individual characters, as well as minor crises, contribute to the meaningful shape of the whole.

The structure is a framework on which the text's life hangs, and the big structural shape is reflected in the lives of characters and the development of themes. Once you have grasped the big structural shape, then, you can use it to help you understand characters and themes by comparing it with the shape of their lives and development. This is what we do in the next step, so at the end of Step 1 we must choose a dominant theme or character to compare with the structure. A dominant theme will be announced in the exposition, and a dominant character will be a central figure in the exposition as well, so you can look back to your summary of the opening and choose who or what to study.

At the beginning of *Othello* the action and discussion centres around the hero's courtship and marriage. Othello arouses envy, resentment, hatred, admiration and love, in Iago, Roderigo, Desdemona's father, the Duke and Desdemona, while his promotion to command Cyprus is the centre of political conversation. In the first act, then, Othello's character dominates the play: everything revolves around him. I will be comparing Othello's character with the three-part structure of *Othello* in the next step, then, because I can see how he dominates the exposition. I will expect to find the shape of the play reflected in what happens to Othello.

2 *Analyse the text*

In this step we want to find out how the structure we have found gives shape to the actual life of the text. Do this simply by comparing the development of the character or theme you have chosen with the three sections of the text in turn. I will look at Othello's character in the exposition, complication and resolution sections of the play. (If I were studying *Othello*, I would already have examined his character before I began to look at the play's structure, so at this stage I am only interested in his overall development.) Keep your thoughts on broad and important points, and keep a distance from the details: just think about your character or theme in general as they are in each section, to bring out the main points.

What stands out about Othello at the beginning of the play? In Act I Othello is successful in every way: Iago's first plot fails, Othello overcomes the objections to his marriage, Desdemona loves him, he is promoted to command Cyprus, and he wins permission to take Desdemona with him. So power and success are the keynotes of his character in the exposition section.

Now look at the complication section. You have studied your character or theme already: what is the main complication or problem which makes up your character or theme in the middle section of the text? This problem will be the main statement you can make about them in the complication section. I have studied Othello and found that his character is divided between love and jealousy. Before he murders Desdemona the tension between these two feelings is extreme, so I can say that this struggle is the main pressure or issue which leads to the crisis. For example, just before killing his wife, Othello says: 'I will kill thee, and love thee after', and 'This sorrow's heavenly, it strikes when it does love' (*Othello*, v.ii.18-22). When I studied his character, then, I found that the key complication in him is a battle between love and jealousy.

Now look at the last section of the text. You know what the key complication was in your character or theme: what happens to this problem in the end? Answering this question will tell you how your character or theme is resolved or comes to a conclusion in the final section. Othello's character is complicated by the struggle between love and jealousy, and jealousy brings about the crisis when he murders Desdemona. What happens afterwards? Her death brings out the truth, Othello learns what a tragic mistake he has made, and his love returns as jealousy is cast out. The resolution of his character is clear: now that jealousy has been cast out his character is not struggling in complications any more and love reigns alone in Othello. Just as at the beginning of the play his love gave him the power to marry Desdemona against her father's and Iago's opposition, so now his love gives him the power to kill himself. Othello's character, then, closely reflects the three sections of the play. In the opening section there is certainty and power; in the complication section there is increasing tension between love and jealousy; in resolution tension disappears and love alone possesses Othello, and he is tragically certain and powerful again.

Step 2 is now complete. What I have done is to relate part of the life in the text, in this case a character, to the three big structural sections. I have used the structure to give me a broader understanding of Othello's character as a whole, and I can see that his life has a clear shape which reflects the overall shape of the play. I have also brought my detached idea of shape down to earth, by relating it to part of the actual life of the text.

3 *Relate the part you have studied to the text as a whole*

Step 2 will have added to your understanding of the structure. First there was only a shape: exposition, complication and resolution. In *Othello*, I can now say that exposition has to do with power and success; complication is full of instability, a conflict between love and jealousy; resolution is power again, but this time a tragic certainty. As usual in Step 3, you are looking for the right kind of leading question which will develop your ideas; and when looking at structure this is easier than usual because you can add to your knowledge by comparing the shape you have found with the times and places in the text. Times and places are important because they are two of the main ways in which a writer gives shape to the world he creates. Life is an endless, shapeless mess and swarms over the whole world. By contrast, a literary text has a beginning and end, and takes place in a limited number of settings. The times and places give the text shape, then, so you can begin this step by surveying these aspects of the text you are studying.

There is no need to reread in detail: you can check your memory of when and where the episodes of the story happen quite easily, by glancing at the beginning of each scene in a play, or the beginning of each chapter in a novel, so you have carried out a brief survey of times and places. While you are glancing through the text, make a note of how much time the events of the story take, and make a list of the most important places in the story, briefly describing the nature or character of each place. Then you will be able to compare your notes on times and places with the three sections of the structure.

I have glanced through the openings of acts and scenes in *Othello*. The play is built around three nights: exposition takes place during one night in Venice. The middle of the play centres on a night in Cyprus, when there is a brawl in the streets and complications build up during the following day. Crisis and resolution happen during the third night. The times in the play, then, closely mirror the three-part structure of the play as a whole and Othello's character. Shakespeare has condensed the vital actions into three chaotic nights, one in each of the three structural sections. All three nights are characterised by plots, confusion, fighting, and people searching for others in the dark.

A survey of places in *Othello* shows that these also reflect the shape of the play. Act I takes place in Venice, but the second and third sections happen in Cyprus. My brief note of what the places are like tells me that Venice is civilised, and the emphasis there is on ordered security under the just rule of the Duke. Cyprus contrasts with Venice, being on the edge of civilisation, threatened by war from the savage Turks. Cyprus emphasises insecurity, then: the main scenes are the sea-port next to a tempestuous sea, and the castle. So complication takes place in an insecure setting dominated by the threat of war. The resolution section changes the setting again, for crisis and resolution take place in the only private place we see in the play: Desdemona's bedchamber. The places in *Othello*, then, also reflect the three-part structure I have found. Exposition is set in the security of Venice, where Othello is secure. Complication happens in the insecurity of Cyprus, where Othello is at war within himself against the savage enemy of jealousy.

Resolution occurs in the privacy of Desdemona's bedchamber, where the secret and intimate truth is revealed.

Times and places generally mirror the structure of a text, so we can confidently compare them with structure in Step 3 as I have done for *Othello*. All we do is look for a reflection of the big structure again. You might, however, be tempted to think that looking at the structure is like adding an arbitrary formula, and that there is no real point in this kind of study. Notice, however, how much my understanding of *Othello* has developed. Not only do I have a better grasp of the overall development of Othello's character; I can also see, now I have looked at the structure, that Venice and Cyprus stand for more than just two places: they signify ideas about stability and insecurity, or civilisation and savagery, which are important motifs in many aspects of the play. The story of one man's struggle with jealousy is given universal significance because it reflects the struggle of civilisation defending itself against savagery in the world as a whole. Now that I have looked at the structure, then, my sense of the text's meaning is much richer and stronger.

STRUCTURE IN MORE COMPLICATED TEXTS

The typical structure I have explained is found in all the novels and plays you may have to study. In long, complicated texts, however, you may find this typical shape repeated several times, or happening twice simultaneously to different groups of characters. In such texts you may find six or nine sections instead of the basic three we found in *Othello*. If you have a complicated text to study, look at the basic shapes in the same way I have shown in this chapter, but use Step 3 differently, to find a unifying thread which holds the whole text together. Study the times and places in Step 3, as before. These will reveal a single thread which joins the different shapes together, no matter how many different groups of characters and events there are.

An example of such a text is *The Rainbow*, by D. H. Lawrence. A brief discussion of this novel shows how Step 3 can be used to find an overall unifying idea. *The Rainbow* tells the stories of three generations of Brangwens: Tom and Lydia Brangwen; their daughter Anna and her husband Will; and the upbringing and love affairs of their daughters, Ursula and Gudrun. There are three generations, different characters brought up in changing times and with different outlooks on life. Each generation provides main characters who are introduced, and whose lives contain their own complications, crises and resolutions. With *The Rainbow* you can analyse each generation as a separate shape in the way I have shown, but the structure of the novel as a whole only becomes clear in Step 3, when you look at the pattern of times and places in the text.

Using the same method I used for *Othello*, I can survey the places in *The Rainbow* and think about what they are like. This time, however, I am looking for something that links them all together. The first generation, Tom and Lydia, live at Marsh Farm, which is an isolated place close to nature: crops, animals and earth. Will and Anna, the second generation, start their married life in a cottage in the small village of Cossethay. When their daughter Ursula is a young woman, she works at Ilkeston, a small industrial town, where industry and poverty are emphasised. The family then moves to Beldover, a suburb in a large industrial district. Ursula and her sister Gudrun both go to college in Nottingham, the big county town. Nottingham represents the real world, having a university, art college, theatres and cinemas. Before the end of the novel, Gudrun feels restricted by Nottingham and wants to move to London.

These sketches of the main places in *The Rainbow* are like the brief descriptions of Venice and Cyprus I noted when we were looking at *Othello*: I am just noting as quickly as possible what each place is like. Now I can think about this list of places, looking for anything they have in common. Does anything about these places link them together, and so hold the several episodes of the novel together? The places in *The Rainbow* are in order of size, showing a single progression: each place is bigger than the last. The novel moves from isolated farmhouse to village to town to suburb to city, and moves the characters steadily outwards into a wider world as it progresses. In Step 3, then, I have found a unifying thread in this complicated novel: there are three generations, several crises, many characters and events, but the places show that there is one movement away from the isolated farm and towards sophisticated modern town society, which is a single, underlying movement, and holds all the different episodes together.

You can use the third step in this way when you are working with a complicated, multiple-structure text. Some element of times or places will help you to grasp the overall shape of the whole, so you can see its broad sweep and gain a richer sense of how the whole text is significant. This provides a wider framework for understanding how different characters and themes, with all their complexities, are arranged to both contribute to, and reflect, the shape of the whole.

STRUCTURE IN POEMS

Poems are often difficult to understand. Many of them are complicated patterns of words, with sudden unexplained images which are difficult to get hold of on first reading. Looking at structure helps you by showing how to divide the poem into sections, work out the main idea of each section, then see how they relate to each other. It is a clear way to start with more difficult poems because a poem is a pattern of words and lines: even when the meaning is difficult, you can often see the pattern and the sections straight away.

In Chapter 1, I said that a poem is like a crisis without the story. Looking at structure makes you divide it into sections, and these are like the different elements of a crisis: they relate to each other and all contribute to the one experience or idea which is expressed by the poem. Think of a poem in the same way as you would think about a crisis: if you can break it down into understandable sections, then see how they relate to each other, you will have a better grasp of its overall meaning.

When you are looking for the structure of a poem, begin by dividing it into parts or sections. A lot of poems show that they are made up of different sections in the way they are set out on the page; so you can see that the first stanza is the first section, the second stanza is the second section, and so on. In some cases, however, the poem you have to study will not show its sections so obviously. If this is the case, look for the natural divisions there are in all kinds of writing: decide where the subject changes, or where the mood or the feelings change. That is the place where a new paragraph would start if it were prose. That is the place, therefore, where one section of the poem ends and another begins. When you have divided a poem into suitable different sections, like the different paragraphs in prose writing, you are well on the way to finding and defining its structure. I shall look at 'The Faithful Swallow', by Thomas Hardy, in some detail, to show how you can find and study the structure of a poem:

'The Faithful Swallow' by Thomas Hardy

When summer shone
Its sweetest on
An August day,
'Here evermore,'
I said, 'I'll stay;
Not go away
To another shore
As fickle they!'

December came:
'Twas not the same!
I did not know
Fidelity
Would serve me so.
Frost, hunger, snow;
And now, ah me,
Too late to go!

(from *Chosen Poems of Thomas Hardy*, Macmillan, 1975, p. 139)

1 *Think about the text*

When you first read a poem you gain some idea of what it is about, even if it is a difficult poem which does not tell you much about the story that led up to it. The first thing to do when you are thinking about the poem, then, is to work out even the most tentative idea of what it is about. This is about a swallow which did not migrate with the other birds, and is now suffering in despair in the cold of winter. Some of the words, such as 'faithful', 'fickle' and 'fidelity', may remind you of the way we talk about love and marriage. Perhaps, then, the poem is about people in love, and uses the swallow as an image. I can work out this much about the poem the first time I read it without having to puzzle anything out. How much you know about a poem from first reading depends on how difficult it is, but you should not cudgel your brains for a long time trying to understand more than is obvious: any brief clue about the poem's subject is enough to be going on with at this stage. The aim is to get an idea of the subject, then move quickly on to find the sections which make up the poem. Look at the poem again, and ask: what are the main sections of this poem?

'The Faithful Swallow' is in two sections. You can see this because it is set out on the page as two stanzas and there is a gap between them. They are the same length and look the same as each other, so they are two equal sections. Step 1 is now complete: I know that the poem is about a swallow's faithfulness which led to misery, and I know that Hardy has organised his idea into two apparently equal sections.

2 *Analyse the text*

In Step 1 you found the sections which make up the poem. Now you want to find out more about the sections. You are looking for an idea of what each section is about, and how they relate to each other, so you can begin by making a brief summary of each section to help you get hold of its main idea. Look for the main or dominant point of each section: even with this seemingly simple poem, each section is eight lines of poetry containing several ideas, so it is quite difficult to keep it all in your head at once. It will be easier to think about the poem as a whole when you have reduced it to a few main points, and that is why it is helpful to summarise. The main ideas expressed by the two sections of 'The Faithful Swallow' are: (i) in the summer fidelity seems right and good, and (ii) when winter comes fidelity has brought suffering and despair.

Now think about these main statements and describe the relationship between them. The different sections of a poem always relate to each other: they are not just bits on their own. You want to describe how they fit together, or what link there is between them. It may help you to have a good idea of how the sections are likely to relate to each other; then you can simply decide which kind of structure there is in the poem you are studying. Most poems will fit one of these three shapes: first, the sections may **contrast** with each other, showing opposite feelings or attitudes. Second, the sections may be stages in the development of an argument or an idea, so each section is a **consequence** of the one before. In such poems you can link your summaries together with logical conjunctions: '*if* (first statement), *then* (second statement)'. Finally, the sections may express slightly different things which are all about the same overall idea, the same feeling or state of mind. You can say that sections like these are **variations** on the poem's idea.

These three kinds of shape tell you what you are likely to find in any poem you have to study. Now you can look at the sections you have found and see which shape best describes how they relate to each other. Does the poem you are looking at bring out a strong contrast? Is it a logical march, leading step by step to a conclusion? Or do the different sections seem to throw light on the same idea, all from different angles? Which of these shapes describes how the two sections of 'The Faithful Swallow' fit together? My summary tells me they are about summer and hope, and winter and despair, so the two sections of this poem contrast with each other. They are set in opposite seasons, and express opposite feelings about fidelity. At this stage I have found the structure of the poem: I have found the sections which make up the poem's shape, summarised each section, and described how the sections relate to each other.

It is worth completing Step 2 by rereading the poem. You have concentrated on main points and ignored details in order to find the structure. Now you can find how the details fit into the bigger pattern, and so develop your understanding of what the poem is about. You will be surprised how much your understanding has grown now that you know the main points and the poem's shape. Phrases or images which were puzzling at first often become clear to you at this stage.

In 'The Faithful Swallow', rereading shows that many other details fit into the contrast structure: on the one side, summer 'shone' its 'sweetest' in 'August'; on the other side, 'December' was 'frost, hunger, snow'. Contempt for other swallows in summer changes to envy of them in the winter. The seasons, emotions and opinions are all part of the basic contrast which gives shape to the poem. My rereading, then, now that I understand the structure, helps me to see what the poem is about: in this case, how it expresses two opposite feelings about life, which I can call hope and despair.

3 Relate the part you have studied to the text as a whole

As usual at the beginning of this step, I want to formulate a leading question which will help me to develop my ideas. I can do this by asking about the structure I have found, and the subject of the poem. What does the poem's idea gain by being structured into this particular shape? 'The Faithful Swallow' is about people's hopes and disappointments, and expresses the contrast between them. Hardy contrasts the bright idealistic hopes people have when they are young with the misery and despair they come to in the end. The sudden opposition between the two stanzas adds to the effect of the poem because it expresses how hope is crushed by cruel experience, very starkly and suddenly. In real life Hardy may have learned the misery of disappointment over many years of slow change as he grew older. In the poem the sharp contrast between the two stanzas heightens the painful-ness of disappointment by making it seem to happen in a moment.

I remarked earlier that the author creates a shapely text out of the mess of actual experience. 'The Faithful Swallow' is a good example of this. The experience Hardy writes about is tragic and destructive: he tells us not to rely on anything, and the experience of the poem is ruinous as all hope is destroyed. The poem, on the other hand, is shapely. Its structure is symmetrical, and we are satisfied by the beauty of its pattern, so Hardy has given a strong shape to a shapeless and destructive experience. Step 3 is now complete. Finding the structure has proved to be a reliable way into looking at the poem, and I now have a clear and growing idea of what it is about.

Looking at 'The Faithful Swallow' has been rewarding, but many poems will be more difficult to analyse. You can see that Hardy's poem is in two fairly equal sections. Half-close your eyes and look at the page, and there are two 'blocks' of text – the two stanzas. The divisions between sections in a poem do not always show themselves in this way. Let us use the same approach, finding the structure of a poem that is printed as a single block of text on the page: a sonnet by Shakespeare.

'Sonnet 52' by William Shakespeare

> . So am I as the rich whose blessed key,
> Can bring him to his sweet up-locked treasure,
> The which he will not ev'ry hour survey,
> For blunting the fine point of seldom pleasure.
> Therefore are feasts so solemn and so rare,
> Since seldom coming in the long year set,
> Like stones of worth they thinly placed are,
> Or captain jewels in the carcanet.
> So is the time that keeps you as my chest,
> Or as the wardrobe which the robe doth hide,
> To make some special instant special blest,
> By new unfolding his imprison'd pride.
>   Blessed are you whose worthiness gives scope,
>   Being had to triumph, being lack'd to hope.
>   (from *The Sonnets, and A Lover's Complaint*, Penguin, 1961, p. 50)

1 *Think about the text*

Having read the poem, you have some idea what it is about. 'Blessed are you' follows 'you as my chest', and the poet mentions 'some special instant special blest'. The poem begins 'So am I rich'. This sonnet must be a love sonnet written to the poet's lover; and some of the words, such as 'rich', 'treasure' and 'jewels', suggest that the poet is expressing something about a priceless and precious thing. Perhaps his lover, or his feeling of love, are being likened to precious things. I have an idea of the poem's subject, so I can now move on to find the sections which make up the poem. Look at the poem again, and ask: what are the main sections which make up this poem?

'Sonnet 52' is less obvious than 'The Faithful Swallow'. The only division obvious to the eye is that the final couplet begins further across than the first twelve lines. Now look at the punctuation. The first twelve lines are three sentences: there are full stops after 'pleasure' (line 4), 'carcanet' (line 8) and 'pride' (line 12). The final couplet is a fourth and final sentence. A lot of poems are like 'Sonnet 52' in that each sentence of the poem can be treated as a different 'section' of the poem. So, if you cannot find the sections as visually separate stanzas, as in 'The Faithful Swallow', look for full stops. Step 1 is now complete. I know that this poem is a love-poem, probably on the theme of the preciousness of love. It is in four sections, each a separate sentence.

2 Analyse the text

You have found the sections which make up the structure of 'Sonnet 52'. Now you want to know more about them, so you summarise each section to bring out its main idea. Remember that you will then define the relationships between the sections. If you allow yourself to look at the words and images too closely at this stage, your mind will fill with the richness of the text, and it will be harder to see the sections and their relationships clearly. The summary, then, has to ignore many details and focus on the central point of each section. The main ideas expressed by the four sections of 'Sonnet 52' are (i) I am like a rich man who sharpens his pleasure by viewing his treasure rarely, (ii) festivals are infrequent for the same reason: to increase our pleasure when they arrive, (iii) the time we are apart is similar, adding to the pleasure of the moment when we meet, and (iv) you are so wonderful that you cause triumph when present and hope when absent.

Now think about these statements and describe how they relate to each other. I said earlier that the relationships between sections in poems are of three kinds. The sections may **contrast** with each other, they may be stages in an argument, so each section is a **consequence** of the one before; or they may all relate to a single overall idea, being **variations** within the poem. Look at the four statements which summarise the sections of 'Sonnet 52', and decide whether contrast, consequence or variation is the best description of the way they fit together in the poem. The second statement is about something which is for 'the same reason' as the first; and the third is about something 'similar'. These three sections, then, are **variations** on the main idea, expressing the lovers' separation from different angles. The first statement is about 'I' and the last is about 'you', so the relationship between these is also of **variation** – a different focus on the same situation, the separation of the lovers. At this stage I have found the structure by finding the sections, summarising each section and describing the relationship between them.

You may be surprised at this result, because on the surface there are a number of logical words which suggest that the sections might be **consequences**. The first three sentences begin with 'So', 'Therefore' and 'So' respectively. The poem also has 'For', 'Since', 'To' and 'By'. There is a strong appearance of logical strucutre, then, but it gives a false impression. In 'Sonnet 52' the word 'So' means 'in the same way', and 'Therefore' means 'for the same reason': these joining words express the relationship between **variations**, not **consequences**. It was important to summarise the sections and define their relationships. Otherwise you might have been misled about the poem's structure. My method, then, has revealed the truth about the structure despite this difficulty.

To complete Step 2, reread the poem. This enables you to see how details fit into the overall shape you have found, and so develop your understanding of what the poem is about. The first section describes the poet as a rich man who avoids viewing his treasure in order to heighten the pleasure when he does. The words build an impression that he is materially and spiritually favoured ('rich' and 'blessed') and there is sensuality in 'sweet' treasure. The idea, on the other hand, is double-edged. Would he become bored if he saw his love too often? (We are not told if his love is a man or a woman.) Is he like a miser? The second section re-expresses the same idea, comparing their meetings to 'feasts', infrequent days of celebration. The religious idea of 'blessed' is continued by 'solemn' feasts which are festivals of worship; and 'rich . . . treasure' becomes 'stones of worth' and 'captain jewels in the carcanet'. The third section is yet another simile for their separation and eventual meeting – his lover is a 'robe' and the time before they meet is his 'wardrobe' in which he keeps his love 'imprison'd'. All three sections describe their meetings, also: 'the fine point of seldom pleasure' in the first; 'so solemn and so rare' in the second, and 'some special instant special blest' in the third. However, in each section there is something unsatisfactory in the poet's idea. I have already commented that the first idea is double-edged. The second mentions 'thinly placed' jewels, making us think there are not enough to go around. The third has overtones of possessive vanity in 'imprison'd pride' and the least pleasing image for his lover as a 'robe'. The fourth section, the final couplet, changes the focus from 'I' to 'you' and praises his love's 'scope', bringing together their partings and meetings in the end because both 'triumph' and 'hope' are happy, positive states of feeling. Again, spiritual worth is in 'blessed' and material success in 'triumph'.

My rereading, then, has helped me to develop a fuller appreciation of 'Sonnet 52'. I was able to notice the details which make up the four sections, and in doing so I began to notice that the feeling expressed in this poem is complex. The poet loves and desires the loved one, but love is a complex, unsatisfactory state; and he portrays himself as a miser (first section) or a callous, vain possessor eager to show off his love, his 'pride' (third section). I also confirmed that the sections are variations, and they are linked by words about religion and material wealth which make a constant motif in the poem. With quite a detailed understanding of the poem, Step 2 is now complete.

3 Relate the part you have studied to the text as a whole

At the beginning of this step, as usual, I want to formulate a leading question which will help me to develop my ideas. I can again do this by asking how the structure enhances the poet's idea. What does the idea gain from being structured into **variations**? 'Sonnet 52' is about the feelings and thoughts of a lover who rarely sees the person he loves. The **variations** structure gives the poet several attempts to express himself. Each is revealing in a different way. Together, they suggest that he cannot express what he feels; and they give the impression that his mind is racing, desperately seeking to rationalise his feelings. The language expresses Shakespeare's love, with its shades of greed and spiritual worship; but the structure expresses his repetitive thoughts, his obsessive concentration on his beloved. The final couplet, my fourth section, also adds to the poem's idea. Throughout the poem Shakespeare has concentrated on himself and sought, vainly, to express his love. The switch to a different focus in the final couplet suddenly enables him to escape from impossible self-expression, and reach a clear, satisfying statement at last. The structure of 'Sonnet 52' enhances the idea, then. Shakespeare's **variations**, expressing the same idea in different versions, convey love as an actual and painful experience as we read the poem. As with 'The Faithful Swallow', we have found that the structure imitates and so intensifies the poet's experience.

The approach I have used here works with poems which are too difficult to approach by finding a theme. It relies upon treating poems as crises from unwritten stories, so you find the elements which together make up the experience the poem conveys. In some poetry, however, these vital elements are expressed in images rather than direct language. You may find the sections and still not understand what they express. It is worth reading the analysis of 'Harry Ploughman' in the next chapter in conjunction with the two approaches to poems I have already explained; then you can study with the confidence that you will be able to find a way into even the most difficult of poems. Remember the discussion of poetry from Chapter 1: poets do not make their experiences live in characters or a story; poetry explains its meaning in any pattern of words which evokes a feeling and communicates the poet's complex idea. It is necessary to be flexible, therefore, in approaching poems. Do not worry if one approach proves unrewarding: try another. Above all, be content to work in steps, because understanding of poetry often comes gradually through repeated rereadings, and with these approaches to guide you, you can afford to wait a little and work methodically to develop your ideas.

CONCLUSION

Perhaps the most important point to make about looking at structure is that it gives you a sense that there is an overall shape to the complex work you are studying. The effect of seeing this overall shape is that all aspects and details of the text, which you began by studying separately, find their places and relate to each other within a grasp of the overall structure. This enriches your understanding enormously, because you can see how different elements work together to create a total effect. Notice, for example, how the chaotic night scenes, the unstable setting of Cyprus, and Othello's struggle in himself all work together to create the tension and disturbing insecurity of the middle acts of *Othello*. A sense of the overall shape, then, enriched by detailed study of different aspects of the text, brings the understanding we have been seeking all along of the text as a complex, but whole and meaningful experience.

These first three chapters have brought us a long way by concentrating on the main elements which help you to understand the text's significance, but I have not yet looked at the very means a writer uses to put his imagined world across to the reader. The author writes, we read. It is all conveyed through language, so we must study and be sensitive to language whenever we are working with literature. It is this matter of looking at the way a text is written, or its *style*, that I will be discussing in the next chapter.

4

Style and imagery

WHAT IS STYLE?

THE style of a text is the way it is written, the language it uses. Studying style enriches your understanding of the text because the style creates the meaning. A short example will show what I mean. Here are two passages which tell the same story:

1. Henderson came in and looked eagerly at his plate. He breathed in a great draught of air. 'Ah, fried egg again! How attractive it looks on a dull morning!'
2. Henderson came in and looked at the plate. The egg looked up at him like a malignant, bloodshot eye. He sighed. 'Ah, fried egg again,' he said flatly. 'How attractive it looks on a dull morning!'

Although the story and Henderson's words are the same in both passages, the meanings are very different. In passage 1 Henderson is cheerful, and we understand that he likes fried eggs. In passage 2 we understand the opposite, that he is speaking sarcastically because the egg looks repulsive to him. The difference lies in the way the two passages are written: different descriptive words ('eagerly', 'flatly') and phrases ('breathed in a great draught of air', 'he sighed'), and the only image ('like a malignant, bloodshot eye'), change the meaning of the passages. I could not understand Henderson without understanding the style. Style, then, is not mere decoration but an essential part of the text.

The rest of this chapter explains how to study a writer's style. Sometimes critics use technical jargon to discuss style, but this is not really necessary: you can analyse and discuss style using your everyday language. In order to come to grips with a writer's language, however, you do have to look closely at the fabric of the text and even at individual words. In particular you have to look at imagery where it occurs, for it is often crucial in revealing the meaning and significance of a work. It is these aspects of style that the following sections discuss.

HOW TO ANALYSE STYLE

Looking at the style of a text is part of the whole process of analysing a work. It is part of what you do in Step 2 when you are closest to the actual fabric of the writing. Obviously, then, before you can look at style you will have gone through the step of finding a crisis and an aspect to focus on. Then decide on a short passage to analyse. The best approach is to focus on just a few lines, as you must be very precise when you analyse style.

'The Wreck of the *Deutschland*' by Gerard Manley Hopkins

To illustrate this, I will use as an example a very difficult poem by Gerard Manley Hopkins called 'The Wreck of the *Deutschland*'. This poem tells the true story of the martyrdom of five nuns, refugees from religious persecution, who were drowned when their ship, the *Deutschland*, was wrecked in a storm. They prayed and welcomed God's power as they died. Hopkins uses this story as a parallel to his own spiritual crisis when he had to come to terms with the apparent cruelty of God and the destructive power of nature. Remember that in order to have come this far in understanding the poem you would already have thought about its theme and chosen a crisis passage where the poet is struggling to understand God's nature. You would therefore have a good sense of the issues involved, but now you need to look more closely at the style to deepen your understanding and appreciation of the text. A rewarding passage to focus on in this poem is the second stanza, which deals with a crisis when Hopkins almost lost his faith:

I did say yes
O at lightning and lashed rod;
Thou heardst me truer than tongue confess
Thy terror, O Christ, O God;
Thou knowest the walls, altar and hour and night:

The swoon of a heart that the sweep and the hurl of thee trod
Hard down with a horror of height:
And the midriff astrain with leaning of, laced with fire of stress.

> (*Poems and Prose of Gerard Manley Hopkins*,
> ed. W. H. Gardner, Penguin, 1979, p. 18)

My immediate response to this stanza is that it is both easy and difficult. It is easy because the overall theme is quite plain: we can see that
the poet is talking about the relationship with God. What makes it difficult is the extraordinary style Hopkins uses; we need to find a way of
describing the language and a way of working out what sense of God
this style creates.

At this point many students panic. It seems so difficult to write
about style, and particularly about such an unusual style as this. You
can make a confident start, however, if you realise that the main things
to look at are the actual words used and the punctuation. There is still
a difficulty, however, because analysing the words involves a new way
of looking at language. You can describe a box easily. You might say,
'It is a long, shiny, silver box, narrow and plain,' or 'It is a large box,
scruffy and rough in old brown leather and covered with straps and
buckles.' The two boxes I have described are very different in shape
and character, but they are easy to describe because the adjectives
come naturally to mind when I look at them. It is easy to describe
what you see, but most people do not describe what they read. When
you analyse words, think of them as if they were things, as if they were
objects you can describe like boxes by saying they are long or short,
dull or shiny, rough or smooth, and so on. Words have size, sound and
character. For example, the words 'love' and 'hate' are respectively
warm and soft, cold and hard. Love means something warm and the 'l'
and 'v' sounds are soft sounds; hate, on the other hand, means something cold, and the hard 't' sound suits the hostility of the word. When
you analyse words, then, describe their effect as if they were objects.

The important words are the verbs, adjectives and common nouns
which the writer uses to create the particular tone and experience he
wants to convey. Look at the stanza from 'The Wreck of the *Deutschland*'. I am going to list the important words, then describe them. The
important words in this stanza are: lightning, lashed, rod, terror, walls,
altar, hour, night, swoon, sweep, hurl, trod, hard, horror, height,
midriff, astrain, leaning, laced, fire, stress. Even from only eight lines of
poetry, I have made a long list of important words. You cannot describe
each one, so you have to find a way of sorting out the list. Either look

for particular words which stand out, or look for groups of words which have some quality in common. In this list I can see three groups of words. There is a group of words about physical pain and violent or punishing action: lashed, rod, swoon, sweep, hurl, trod, hard, fire, stress. A second group is made up of words of fear: terror, swoon, horror. Finally, there are some words about the grandeur and power of nature: lightning, height, fire. Once you have sorted out the words, try to describe them. For example, the first group of words, which are violent and hurtful, are all short: they are sudden words like blows which hit the poem. These are the important words in the stanza and clearly form the largest group. There is no need to describe every group. What I am seeking to do is to define the most significant aspect of the style. I have achieved that by describing its violent physical language.

Now look at the punctuation of the stanza. Punctuation is a useful aid to analysing style because it tells you about the rhythm and speed of the language in the passage you are analysing. Smooth even pace goes with balance and calm; a rushing, fast rhythm goes with excitement and hysteria; and broken, halting rhythm indicates disturbance, uncertainty and confusion. Your aim is to work out the speed and rhythm of the passage you are analysing, then to compare this with what it is about to see how the rhythm reveals the moods of the text. A lot of elements govern how fast or slowly the writing flows, but you can use punctuation as a sure straightforward guide to the points you want to find. You are only interested in strong feelings, so you can ignore regularly-spaced punctuation. You want to find where strong feelings make the writing rush, or break it up into short phrases. These places are like crises in the style: they show where feelings and tensions break out, or where the mood changes. Look through the passage and pick out places where there is a lot of punctuation which breaks up the writing into little bits, or where an unusually long gap between punctuation makes the writing rush along uninterrupted. In the stanza I am analysing, lines 6 and 7 have no punctuation at all: an unusually long single phrase which takes a deep breath to read through, and reads very fast. These two lines are a crisis in the stanza. Hopkins describes how God seemed to tread his heart down with unimaginable power. This is the central terrifying experience of God's power which Hopkins underwent, and the headlong speed of these two lines creates Hopkins's spiritual crisis.

You can analyse the words and punctuation of any passage in the same way that I have shown in this example. The crucial point to grasp is that we do this sort of analysis so as to get closer to the meaning of the text and how that meaning is created. As a result of my analysis, I feel that I now have a sharper sense of how Hopkins is afraid of God and how God can appear terrifying in his power and cruelty. This impression is created by Hopkins's words which portray violent action and pain. The relationship between style and subject, then, is very clear: Hopkins creates the power and cruelty of God in a style filled with violent action and fear. In lines 6 and 7 the poetry is a rush of words of violent pain which hurtles along at high speed. These lines describe Hopkins's experience of being crushed or thrown down by God's power. The style, then, creates the subject by evoking feelings of fear and pain in the reader, and the short words hit at us as we read, like the lash of a punishing God.

The aim of studying style is to enrich your understanding of the text, so you should never discuss the style unless you can show how it creates the complex reality of the world of the text. It is not enough to just list words without discussing them: words have sound, size, and carry rich meaning which you have to describe. You must not merely count the commas, either: the punctuation in a text tells you how to read it, revealing its speed, its rhythm, whether it is broken or rushes on. Studying style, then, involves thinking carefully about how the language creates the meaning and effect of the text. Central to any discussion of style, however, is an understanding of how writers use imagery.

HOW IMAGERY WORKS

Imagery occurs wherever there is a comparison between something which is actually there in the story, and something else. For example, when you say 'he is as strong as an ox', 'he' (who is part of the story, and so actual) is compared with an ox (which is imagined for the sake of the comparison, so it is not actual). Each comparison is called an **image** or a **figure**, so the words which make the comparison are **figurative language**. A lot of ordinary language is figurative: '*He led her a merry dance* for a few months, then *dropped her like a stone*'. 'When she saw him again two years later, the experience *reopened every wound in her heart*'. It is difficult to write or speak in English without comparing something actual with something imagined.

The imagery you analyse in literature is, however, different from this casual playing with language which occurs in everyday conversations. Whenever there is an image in a text, something which is not actually there in the story is brought into the world of the text. When the poet writes 'My love is like a red, red rose', there is no rose in the actual situation, only a woman. On the other hand, the image-idea of a 'red, red rose' is part of the poem. It is part of our experience as we read, and the poet has put it there to be part of the pattern he creates. Think of an image as an idea added into the world of the text in this way. Everything in the text contributes to its world. Images, or the figurative ideas a writer adds, are just the same as all the other ideas in a text: they are part of the pattern you study to understand. Imagery is not there merely to ornament the text but to add ideas which the writer wants to add. It follows that images add to your understanding of characters, themes or whatever they apply to, and you study them to help you understand the text. When you study an image, then, you want to discover two things: how the comparison helps to explain the actual thing it is compared with in the text, and how the added image-idea expands the meaning of the text.

Romeo and Juliet by William Shakespeare

I shall demonstrate how you can analyse imagery using examples from Shakespeare's *Romeo and Juliet*. Analysing imagery, like analysing style, is part of our overall method, so by this stage I would have already established a number of points. I would have read the play and become interested in love, which is a major theme as the opening of the play makes clear. Here is how the story starts: Romeo is in love with Rosaline, who swears she will never marry. Then he falls in love with Juliet. After their first meeting, Romeo climbs into the orchard of Juliet's father's house, and Juliet appears on a balcony above him. The famous 'balcony scene' follows, where they declare their love for each other and agree to marry secretly the next day.

Certain questions are prompted by this summary of the play's opening: how is it that Romeo can be in love with two different girls in quick succession? How and why do his feelings suddenly change? In order to pursue the theme and these questions about love I would have to focus on a specific crisis episode, such as the balcony scene where Romeo and Juliet openly declare their love for each other. By this stage, then, thinking about the text and looking at the crisis scene should have given me a good sense of the issues in the play.

Now, however, I want to look more closely at a single speech from within the crisis scene, as this will add to my understanding of how Shakespeare uses his language to create the meaning of the play. I could look at one speech in the same way as illustrated in the last section, showing how the style creates the meaning, but I have noticed that poetry is particularly rich in imagery, so I can narrow my focus rather more and concentrate on this. I want to know how the imagery helps to reveal Romeo's feelings, and what the image-ideas themselves add to the world of the play. Here is an extract from Romeo's speech as Juliet appears on the balcony:

> But, soft! What light through yonder window breaks?
> It is the east, and Juliet is the sun.
> Arise, fair sun, and kill the envious moon,
> Who is already sick and pale with grief
> That thou her maid art far more fair than she.
> Be not her maid, since she is envious;
> Her vestal livery is but sick and green,
> And none but fools do wear it; cast it off.
>   (*Romeo and Juliet*, II.ii.2-9, The Complete Works, Collins, 1964)

The first task is to find and define the images: say what actual thing in the text is being compared to what imagined thing. The first comparison I can find in this speech is a comparison between Juliet and the sunrise in the second line: 'It is the east, and Juliet is the sun.' I know, then, that Juliet is compared to the sun. Now reread the rest of the extract. Notice that Shakespeare begins with a straightforward comparison between Juliet and the sun, then develops the idea in the next six lines. This is common in literary imagery; a simple comparison is rare, so it is always worth looking for further elaboration of the image-idea. The method you use has to take this into account, so after defining the original image (Juliet = the sun), carry on defining the comparison as it is developed and added to in the rest of the passage.

In the passage we are studying, the image-idea is developed a lot. In the third line, Romeo introduces the idea of the moon, and in lines 4/5 he elaborates on the idea by describing the moon as 'sick' and 'pale' and envious of the beauty and brightness of the sun. If the image you are analysing develops in this way, you have to write a full description of each side of the comparison, that is the actual situation and the image-idea, so you can see clearly how they relate to each other. The actual situation while Romeo speaks is this: Romeo has a new strong feeling of love for Juliet, which has displaced the older weaker love he felt before for Rosaline. Romeo wants Juliet to respond to his love, so this new feeling can fill his life. Rosaline did not respond because she had sworn to be chaste and never marry. The image-idea relates to this situation in a number of ways. Here is an account of the image-idea: the sun is about to rise in the east so dazzlingly bright that it will 'kill' the fading light of the moon. The moon is older, and is jealous that the young sun is already more fair. The moon's light is greenish-white, the greenness standing for jealousy and sickness, the pale whiteness described as 'vestal' referring to Roman priestesses famous for their chastity. Romeo wants the sun to 'cast off' this virginal and sick light, which will disappear in the presence of the sun's brightness.

These two descriptions of the situation, one a plain account of the actual situation and the other an account of Romeo's image-idea, relate to each other closely. Juliet is the sun, the new bright light in Romeo's life. The old weaker light in Romeo's life is Rosaline, so the pale moon comes to represent her. Romeo is still bitter about Rosaline's chastity – the moon's 'vestal livery' – and urges Juliet to cast off chastity and respond to his passion. The image-idea therefore expresses the state of Romeo's feelings at this crisis-point of change from one love to another. The comparison of the sun's brightness against the pallor of the moon helps us to understand how he can forget one love and fall in love so quickly and strongly again.

I have now analysed the image in Romeo's speech by describing both sides of the comparison fully, then thinking about how they relate to each other. I said that there are two questions to answer when you analyse imagery: what does the image add to your understanding of the actual situation, and what does the image-idea add to the world of the text? I can now answer the first of these questions. The image helps us to understand the sudden change in Romeo's feelings. It explains to us that the two kinds of 'love' Romeo has felt are completely different feelings, and that his love for Juliet is much stronger than anything he felt for Rosaline before. His former love is as insignificant beside the power of his new love as the light of the moon when eclipsed by the light of the sun. This in turn helps me to understand the theme of love in the play. Clearly Shakespeare is presenting two completely different feelings, one sick and pale, the other strong and bright, and both are called 'love'.

I can now consider the second question: what does the image-idea add to the world of the text? In other words, how does it expand the experience of the play? This might seem a difficult question to answer, but really it is straightforward. Imagery always works to expand the scope of the text and relate it to larger ideas. The result is that the text takes on a larger significance and we see it as being about more than just the lives and actions of a few characters.

The passage we are looking at is a clear example of this effect. The image reminds us that the actual experience of one boy and girl in Verona is part of a wider experience which is common to all of us, and which can be called **universal**. The reader does not know Juliet: she is only one girl, no more or less important than any of the millions of 13-year-old girls in the world. On the other hand, all readers know the sun, which is the source of daylight and life for the world. The sun's beauty and importance is part of a universal experience, so the image connects the **particular**, the beauty of one young girl in Verona, with the **universal**, the warmth and light of the life-giving sun. By making this connection in his imagery, Shakespeare makes Juliet's beauty and Romeo's feelings about her significant. The story which is being played out on stage becomes enormously important: as important as the sun.

I have now analysed how Romeo's image works, and I can answer both the questions with which I began. First, the contrast of the sun and the moon explains the two different feelings Romeo calls 'love'; second, by connecting Romeo's particular feelings with the universal power of nature in the sun, the image reminds us that Romeo's love is part of a wider, significant and grandiose process in life and nature: it reminds us that love itself is a powerful force in human beings. Can you see, then, that imagery works on two levels? First, it illuminates the particular situation, the particular crisis the characters find themselves in; second, it expands the text, giving it a universal significance. This idea of texts as universal is important and some further discussion here may help you and also provide some useful tips about what to look for.

We live in a technological world. The seasons and the cycles of plant and crop life do not matter to us so much any more: modern equipment like central heating, air-conditioning and electric light protect us from their influence, and we can buy most fresh produce all the year round. Belief in God is also less important in modern society, for this century has seen the growth of atheism and indifference. Finally, the old order of society has crumbled, and we are brought up to think of ourselves as equals, rather than to think of society as a ladder on which every person has a known position somewhere between king and beggar. You are a present-day student. Most of the texts you study, on the other hand, were written when natural cycles, religion and a rigid social structure were all supremely important factors in everyday life. These *universal* factors in life are the common material of imagery in the texts you study.

You will find these hints on the universal particularly useful when you study imagery in poetry. Many poems simply refer to this context and assume that the reader will understand and respond to the poet's implication. Looking for references to nature, religion and social order may provide you with the key which will help you to understand an otherwise baffling poem. Remember 'The Faithful Swallow', by Thomas Hardy, which I used as an example in Chapter 3. I found that the structure of Hardy's poem was based on a contrast between summer and winter, which was also a contrast between youth, hope and faithful love (summer), and old age, despair, misery and loss (winter). Hardy, then, was using a reference to the seasons to put his poem into a universal context where hope and despair, youth and old age, summer and winter, are all involved in a big cycle of life which the reader is expected to share and understand. When you study imagery in literature, think about the universal context of the world we live in: this will help you to understand how the imagery connects the text with universal forces, and so imbues individual characters and events with added significance.

We have looked at an image from one chosen crisis passage. A significant image like this comparing Juliet and the sun, however, usually recurs, coming up repeatedly in different situations at different times, just like the themes in texts. Because images recur you can expect them to add considerably to your understanding of a text. In order to study an image further, use the method I have used before in Step 3: that is, think logically about the text and decide where else the same image is likely to occur. Your aim is to confirm what you found from your first crisis passage, and, from additional passages, to gain additional understanding of how the imagery works. In this case I am studying the comparison of Juliet to the dazzling light of the sun. I found this image in a speech where Romeo describes Juliet; it seems likely that the image will appear again in other places where Romeo describes Juliet. All I have to do is to choose two such places, if possible one before and another after the crisis I first looked at.

This is quite easy: when Romeo first sees Juliet, he describes her, and he describes her again at the end of the play just before he dies. All I have to do is to reread these two passages and pick out any images which compare Juliet with a dazzling brightness and light. So, when Romeo first sees Juliet, he says:

> O, she doth teach the torches to burn bright!
> It seems she hangs upon the cheek of night
> As a rich jewel in an Ethiop's ear –

(I.v.42-4)

As before, define the image: in these lines Romeo says that Juliet is a brighter light than the torches which light the room; she is like a star, bright against the night sky like a jewel shining against the black skin of an Ethiopian. These images confirm that the comparison between Juliet and brightness which I found in the first passage occurs here as well. In both cases Juliet is compared with light, and is contrasted with the paleness or darkness which surrounds her. The next task is to make an exact comparison between the two passages: you know that they are the same kind of image, but is there any difference between them which will add to your understanding of the text? In this case there is. When Romeo first sees Juliet she is brighter than torches, then she is a star. By the time he sees her in the 'balcony scene' she is the sun, far brighter than torches or stars. The difference between the two passages tells us that the power of Romeo's love for Juliet grows enormously between his first seeing her, and his second meeting with her later the same night. Looking at this passage, then, has confirmed that images of light for Juliet are a recurrent motif in the text and revealed more about how Romeo's feeling of love develops and grows in power.

The second passage I have chosen to look at, in following up this image, is near the end of the play. Romeo enters a tomb and sees Juliet apparently dead. When he sees Juliet's 'body', Romeo says:

> For here lies Juliet, and her beauty makes
> This vault a feasting presence full of light.

(V.iii.85-6)

Romeo uses an image of light again here, which further confirms that the connection between Juliet and brightness runs throughout the text. In this case Juliet's 'light' is described as more powerful than death or the grave. In other words, her light has grown stronger still, and can overcome even death, the ultimate darkness. Looking at another passage has confirmed what I found at first, and added to my understanding.

These images from *Romeo and Juliet* show something else about the way imagery works: when one kind of image occurs repeatedly in the text you are studying, it is likely to develop in the same way that characters and themes develop. At this stage you have three definitions of the image you are studying: one from early in the text, one from your first chosen crisis, and one from later in the text. Look for the way the image-ideas develop through the three examples you have found. You can do this by putting the three image-ideas together in sequence so they make a sort of image story. Romeo's images for Juliet make a story like this: first she is brighter than torches, she is like a star; then she is the sun, lighting the world; and finally she is a light powerful enough to overcome death. This sequence tells the story of the power of Juliet's beauty and Romeo's love for her. The images help us to understand how the power of love grows throughout the play, until it is finally more important even than death.

This analysis of *Romeo and Juliet* shows how richly rewarding the study of images can be. It also demonstrates the point I made earlier: images are not mere decorative extras. Think of them as ideas woven into the pattern of the text, rather like themes, which can develop inside the actual story; they are part of the world of the text, to be studied and understood in their own right.

IMAGERY IN SHORTER POEMS

I have said that poems are like the crises from unwritten stories. Narrative, description, dialogue and explanation are left out. Instead, the poet compresses different elements of a crisis into a condensed, pure form. In many poems, however, the first reading gives only a vague impression of what the poem is about. I have shown how you can find a way into understanding poems by finding a theme (Chapter 1) or finding the poem's structure (Chapter 3). But some poems use imagery as the main form of communication; and because poems are so condensed, it may be difficult to analyse a theme or the structure unless you understand the imagery first.

Remind yourself of the explanation of **imagery** on page 66. Some poems consist almost entirely of **figurative language**. It stands for thoughts, feelings, a pattern of ideas; but because the image-ideas are all you to have to go on, it is hard to find the actual thing which was the origin of the comparison. The solution to this problem is to find a pattern in the **imagery**. The pattern you find in the imagery, like the pattern in a poem's structure, will provide you with a way in to understanding the poet's idea. I can demonstrate this by tackling a poem which, at first sight, is very confusing indeed. I have deliberately chosen a Hopkins poem again because of the obvious complexity of his work on first reading.

'Harry Ploughman' by Gerard Manley Hopkins

Hard as hurdle arms, with a broth of goldish flue
Breathed round; the rack of ribs; the scooped flank; lank
Rope-over thigh; knee-nave; and barrelled shank –
    Head and foot, shoulder and shank –
By a grey eye's heed steered well, one crew, fall to;
Stand at stress. Each limb's barrowy brawn, his thew
That onewhere curded, onewhere sucked or sank –
    Soared or sank –
Though as a beechbole firm, finds his, as at a rollcall, rank
And features, in flesh, what deed he each must do –
    His sinew-service where do.

He leans to it, Harry bends, look. Back, elbow, and liquid waist
In him, all quail to the wallowing o' the plough. 'S cheek crimsons; curls
Wag or crossbridle, in a wind lifted, windlaced –
    See his wind-lilylocks-laced;
Churlsgrace, too, child of Amansstrength, how it hangs or hurls
Them – broad in bluff hide his frowning feet lashed! raced
With, along them, cragiron under and cold furls –
    With-a-fountain's shining-shot furls.
            (from *The Poems of Gerard Manley Hopkins*, OUP, 1967, p. 104)

1 *Think about the text*

The title tells us that this poem is about a man called Harry who is ploughing. This is confirmed by 'He leans to it, Harry bends' and 'the wallowing o' the plough'. After reading the poem for the first time, your mind may be buzzing with impressions and associations; but you are likely to be confused by the oddness of the style: the title is almost all you can really say that you understand. There is no need to panic at this point. Remember, any small understanding you find will be enough to make a start. Try the two methods of approaching poetry I have demonstrated earlier in this book. Can you find a theme? In this poem there are several words for parts of the body, such as 'head', 'foot', 'shoulder', 'waist', 'limb', 'sinew' and 'back'. The poem is about a ploughman, and there is a lot in it about physical work. Physical work is probably a **theme** of this poem. Next, can you divide the poem into sections in order to find its **structure**? Yes, you can. The poem is divided into two main sections, with a gap between 'His sinew-service where do', and 'He leans. . . .'

Even with this confusing, intimidating poem, you have succeeded in completing Step 1. You have an idea of a theme of the poem which you can pursue in Step 2; and you have found the two main sections of the poem, so the structure may also help you to develop your understanding during the analysis stage. Notice that our method has followed the same principle as before: concentrate on what you *do* understand, however little it may be at first. That is what you have to build on. If you allow yourself to concentrate on what you do *not* understand, you may start to guess wildly.

2 *Analyse the text*

In this step you want to find out more about the theme, and possibly about the structure as well. You found a theme of physical work, so follow the method demonstrated in Chapter 1, rereading the poem and looking for ideas, descriptions, comments about physical work. With 'Harry Ploughman', however, you may well discover little more from rereading the poem, even if you conscientiously look up the meanings of rare words such as 'flue' (down, or fluff), 'curded' (coagulated, solidified from a liquid state), 'Churlsgrace' (the grace of a 'churl' or peasant) and 'Amansstrength' (oh! a man's strength, of course!). However, you do notice that there are a lot of images, starting with the simile in the opening phrase: 'Hard as hurdle arms'. So rereading the poem has not helped you to complete Step 2 by analysing the theme; but it has revealed that there is a wealth of imagery to study.

With many poems you will be able to pursue either a theme or the structure, and the images in those poems will often become clear as you work through our three steps. In the case of 'Harry Ploughman', however, I am not confident of making headway until I understand more about the imagery. Adopt a different method with poems like this one, therefore. First, make a list of the images in the poem, using the words 'compared to' in each case to explain the comparison. I shall do this for 'Harry Ploughman' now:

1. Arms compared to 'hurdle' (woven fences)
2. Downy hair on his arms compared to 'broth' (soup)
3. His ribs compared to a rack
4. The tendons on his thigh compared to rope
5. Part of his knee (the hollow behind?) compared to a nave, the colonnaded main part of a church
6. His 'shank' (the lower half of his leg) compared to a barrel
7. His whole body compared to a ship, his eye the helmsman ('steered well, one crew, fall to')
8. Each of his limbs compared to a barrow (an ancient burial mound)
9. His 'thew' (vigour, muscles) compared to (a) a solidifying and then a flowing liquid, and (b) the trunk of a beech-tree
10. The different parts of him compared to soldiers being called to duty at a 'rollcall'
11. His waist compared to liquid
12. The wind compared to a lace-maker, making lace with his hair
13. The peasant's 'grace' compared to the child of his man's strength
14. His hair compared to lilies
15. His feet compared to a face frowning
16. The earth curling from the plough-blade compared to a fountain, its drops shining (in the sun?)

I have made a list of images from 'Harry Ploughman'. I looked through the poem, and each time I came to an image I decided what the comparison was and wrote it down in my 'notes' list. This is similar to the way I analysed structure by using summaries: it is easier to see structure in a few clear statements than by looking at the complexity of the poem itself. With imagery, it is easier to see a pattern in the images if you make a clear list of them, lifting them out of the baffling complexity of the text.

Now turn your attention to the list. Look for any pattern. You are likely to find one of three kinds of pattern, or combinations of them. First, the images may **develop** like an **image-story**. I noticed this effect in the example from *Romeo and Juliet*: Romeo's images for Juliet were of light, and became brighter and more powerful as the play progressed, telling the **image-story** of the ever-growing power of Romeo's love. Secondly, the images may be classified into **groups of images** which have something in common with each other. Finally, there may be an image which appears more than once, or is **recurrent**. When you find any of these patterns in your list of imagery, you have made a vital step towards fully understanding the poem. A pattern gives you a larger unit than a single image: it is greater than a single image, which may be only a minor detail. The pattern is an important element in the poem's idea.

My list of images from 'Harry Ploughman' shows the second type of pattern. I can classify many of them into **groups of images** which have something in common. I shall list them in their groups here, for the sake of clarity. It is not necessary for you to do this when you work on a poem. Simply find what they have in common and group them in your mind.

Group 1: solid things compared to liquids
2. Downy hair on his arms compared to 'broth' (soup)
9. His 'thew' (vigour, muscles) compared to a solidifying and flowing liquid
11. His waist compared to liquid
16. The earth curling from the plough-blade compared to a fountain, its drops shining (in the sun?)

Group 2: solid, work and farm objects
1. Arms compared to 'hurdle' (woven fences)
3. His ribs compared to a rack
4. The tendons on his thigh compared to rope
5. Part of his knee (the hollow behind?) compared to a nave, the colonnaded main part of a church
6. His 'shank' (the lower half of his leg) compared to a barrel
8. Each of his limbs compared to a barrow (an ancient burial mound)
9. His 'thew' (vigour, muscles) compared to trunk of a beech-tree

Group 3: ideas of a team, different individuals working together for one purpose
7. His whole body compared to a ship, his eye the helmsman ('steered well, one crew, fall to')
10. The different parts of him compared to soldiers being called to duty at a 'rollcall'

Group 4: white or bright and delicate things
12. The wind compared to a lace-maker, making lace with his hair
14. His hair compared to lilies

16. The earth curling from the plough-blade compared to a fountain, its drops shining (in the sun?)

One other image, not part of a group
13. The peasant's 'grace' compared to the child of his man's strength

These **groups of images** tell you something about the poet's main ideas when describing Harry the ploughman. Develop your ideas by describing each group of images you have found, and saying where the group is in the poem. Each statement you make is significant and secure because the images you have listed and grouped are the textual evidence to support it. In the case of 'Harry Ploughman', I can now make several statements about the poem.

There are images of solid things as flowing liquid throughout the poem, including one in the first line and one in the last line. One of these images (no. 9) seems to emphasise liquid changing into solid and back into liquid again. Hopkins evidently wants the reader to appreciate the flowing movement as Harry works, and eventually the flowing movement of the earth produced by Harry's work. There are images of strong, solid objects such as 'hurdle', 'rope' and 'barrel', and of solid and massive objects such as 'nave' and 'barrow'. These images are all in the first section of the poem. Hopkins evidently wants the reader to have a vivid idea of Harry's massiveness and the barrel-barrow-tree-trunk-like shape of his muscles. There are images of teamwork between parts, of a ship's crew and an army unit. Hopkins conveys Harry's coordination and his skill at work in these images. Finally, there are images of delicate and shining things such as 'lace' and 'lilies' and the shining spray of a fountain. These are all found in the second section of the poem.

A look at these statements shows that I have come a long way in understanding 'Harry Ploughman'. Analysing imagery has helped me to make a breakthrough with this difficult poem. Also, looking at the statements I have made about groups of images shows that solid, hard images are confined to the first section of the poem, while delicate and bright images take over in the second section. This suggests an **image-story** that I did not notice at first because of the many other details in the poem. The story seems to begin with Harry's physical strength and work, hard work with rough, homely materials; and ends with lace, lilies and fountains, beautiful and delicate. In short, out of hard work comes delicate beauty. This **image-story** is a clue to the poet's central idea.

Step 2 has been immensely rewarding, but before you move on to Step 3, look back at the small understanding of theme and structure I had at the beginning of Step 2. I knew that physical work is a theme of 'Harry Ploughman'. What does the poem say about physical work? My analysis of images has answered this question: the poet shows physical work as full of graceful, liquid movement; expresses wonder at the strength and physique of the labourer; admires his coordination and skill; and suggests that physical work can produce beauty equivalent to the most delicate productions of nature (lilies) or craft (lace). On structure, I had noticed the poem's two sections. Can I say more about these sections? Here, I am less sure of the answer, but analysing imagery has provided a hint: the first section emphasises the solid, hard and strong. The second section emphasises delicacy and brightness. Step 2 is now complete. I listed the images, looked for a pattern in my list of images, and made statements describing the pattern of images in the poem. Then I thought about my initial ideas of theme and structure, and developed these ideas using the imagery-statements as a guide. I now have a rich and growing understanding of 'Harry Ploughman'.

3 *Relate the part you have studied to the text as a whole*

As usual, I want to formulate a leading question, which will further develop my ideas. Think about what you have done by this stage: you have concentrated on the **images** and analysed them, but you have hardly thought about the **actual meaning** of the poem. The sensible question to ask, then, is: how do the images relate to the actual meaning of the poem?

First, what do I know about the actual meaning of 'Harry Ploughman'? I know that it is about a ploughman at his work. The first section seems to be descriptive: the poet conveys his impression of Harry at work. The second section begins with an action: Harry 'leans to it, Harry bends'. As far as I can tell at this stage, something called 'Churlsgrace' which is the child of 'Amansstrength' then 'hurls'. The sentence is confusing, so it is hard to work out what 'Churlsgrace' hurls; but it seems that his grace throws his feet as he walks behind the plough, and also throws the earth aside from the plough-blade. So the poem describes Harry and shows the ploughman's strength pushing, 'hurling' his feet and the earth along.

Now put the actual meaning with my conclusions from analysing the imagery. The imagery changes from rough and solid to delicate and fragile; and from dark and earthy to bright and white. If I relate the imagery to the meaning, I can see that the actual meaning is not the most important thing. The poet is not moved by the fact that the plough hurls earth. He is moved by the creation of beauty, expressed in the **image** for the earth, 'With-a-fountain's shining-shot furls'. Also, I found that the imagery is in contrasting groups: solid, liquid; hard, soft. This helps me to understand the odd word Hopkins has invented, 'Churlsgrace'. A churl is a peasant and our impression is of a rough and earthy person, in contrast to 'grace' which brings to mind elegance, delicacy and also (in its religious sense) God's love. Putting the contrasts of imagery and the meaning together, then, tells me that the poem is about the way contrasting things can be brought together and work together to produce shining beauty. The images of an army unit and 'one crew' emphasise this point.

There is a lot more to discover about 'Harry Ploughman', of course; but it has amply demonstrated that you can use the imagery in a poem to throw light on its meaning: I have reached a firm understanding of Gerard Manley Hopkins's purpose in writing the poem. In this book I have shown three different ways of approaching poems: by **finding a theme**, by **finding the structure**, and by **analysing the imagery**. This is because poems often give you very little to go on, so approaching unseen poetry is one of the most intimidating tasks literature students face. Remember to be flexible in your approach: try one method, but if it does not work do not lose heart. Try another method instead. Notice my approach to 'Harry Ploughman'. I made use of elements of all three methods, to get at the poem's idea. The **theme** method gave a little help at first, and I returned to it after working on **imagery**. The **structure** method did not give any help at first, but the poem's two sections were a helpful idea at the end of Step 2 and in Step 3. Go forward confidently, then. As you practise approaching different poems, you can confidently begin by applying the methods I have demonstrated. As you become more experienced you will find that you can combine the different approaches I have described; and you will find that you switch from one to another or use all three simultaneously. Understanding poetry will become less laborious, faster, and more and more satisfying.

Finally, think back to the example of Henderson and his fried egg with which I began this chapter. The example showed that you cannot understand the writer's meaning without understanding the style. The same is true of 'Harry Ploughman'. The style of the poem – its imagery – contains vital clues to the poet's idea. In fact, with the loose syntax of the first section, and the confusing sentence at the end, you can say that the meaning of 'Harry Ploughman' resides more in the images than in any other aspect of the poem. This underlines the point of Henderson's egg, which is the point of this chapter: that style and meaning are interrelated, and contribute vitally to each other.

CONCLUSION

There is nothing mysterious about analysing style: do not be put off by the long, technical-sounding words which some professional critics use. Literature is about the complexity of ordinary life, and you can use your ordinary knowledge of life and language to understand how the style and imagery work. The examples I have discussed show how informative this study can be as long as you focus closely enough on important selected passages from the crises you have chosen to study. This short chapter can only help you to begin looking at style and imagery, but the approach I have explained will hold good for all texts. Essentially it is a matter of looking carefully at the actual words used and thinking about how they help create the meaning of the text. This, in many cases, is really no more than stating the obvious: if the words are all to do with fear or pain then this adds to our sense of something unpleasant or terrifying; if the sentences seem short or broken then this creates a sense of something disjointed or troubled. If you focus on an image, try to see how it illuminates the subject matter of the text, but also how it adds weight and significance to the text, giving it a universal meaning relevant to all of us. Once again this is usually a case of stating the obvious, pointing out how the images give the work universality by connecting it with the larger processes of nature. The central thing to remember is that you cannot discuss the language of a text without discussing the meaning of that text. If you consistently make the connection between style and meaning, then your discussion will always be developing in the right direction.

5

Irony

WHAT IS IRONY

LITERATURE is complex. This means that you cannot take a single view of it. In literature as in real life there are always two or more sides to a question because the complexity of different elements makes up reality. When you read factual writing you expect it to tell you one kind of truth or to express one point of view. Literature is different: it presents the complex nature of reality. So, for example, you cannot say that the painful side of love in *Wuthering Heights* (see Chapter 1) is 'wrong' because it is a real part of the world of the text, just as real as the affection and attraction which are also part of love in the text. When you study literature, then, you have to accept the complex nature of reality and understand two or more sides to every experience. The earlier chapters of this book have shown how to find and define the complexity of a text; this chapter is about the effect of this complexity, which is called irony.

It is difficult to grasp what irony means, but here is a working definition of it which should become clearer in the next section and as you read the examples. Irony exists where there are two or more related meanings or attitudes to be understood from what is written in the text. These two meanings could seem to contradict each other; yet the text not only suggests both meanings, but also suggests that they both have some validity. Irony is the relationship between these different meanings and attitudes in a work of literature.

WHAT IRONY IS NOT

Irony is not sarcasm. In sarcasm there are two meanings at first, but you quickly realise that one of the meanings is ludicrous. For example, if you spill coffee over the white sitting-room carpet and your father says, 'Well done, that was brilliant!' there are apparently two meanings: first what your father says (well done), then what he means (you clumsy oaf). Your father is being sarcastic: he says the opposite of what he means in order to ridicule your mistake. He does not mean 'well done' at all: There is only one real meaning, 'you clumsy oaf', so there is no irony.

Irony is not ambiguity. Ambiguity occurs when you cannot decide what the truth is because you do not have enough information. For example, you are invited to two parties on the same evening. Next morning a friend asks, 'Where did you go last night?' and you answer, 'I went out'. You do not want to tell your friend which party you chose. There are two possible meanings and no way of telling which one is true: you are being ambiguous. With ambiguity, then, there is no relationship between the two possible meanings; with sarcasm there is only one real meaning. Look at our definition of irony again: irony exists where the meanings are all valid (so it is not sarcasm), and where there is a relationship between the different meanings (so it is not ambiguity). Now we have looked at two kinds of double meaning which are not irony, I can explain in more detail what irony is.

WHAT TO DO WHEN YOU FIND IRONY

Finding irony means finding two significant versions of the truth, or two attitudes to the same thing which are both valid. You will come across irony while you are engaged in studying other aspects of the text. The examples which follow show that irony is found everywhere in literature: in a word, a sentence, or in the structure, plot or themes of a whole text. I will start with the irony which we notice in the individual words of a text. My example comes from Shakespeare's *Hamlet*. Hamlet is prince of Denmark. His father is poisoned by his uncle Claudius, who then becomes king and quickly marries Gertrude, Hamlet's mother. The play tells the story of Hamlet's revenge on Claudius for the murder of his father. Throughout the play Hamlet himself is racked by doubt and filled with disgust at his mother for marrying Claudius. Hamlet is also disgusted at humanity in general, including himself, and repeatedly thinks about suicide. He looks for purity and is concerned with what is right. Other people easily forget what is right: they compromise and find self-justifying excuses for their faults. Hamlet is different because he cannot excuse himself or anyone else for being ordinary sinful human beings.

Let us assume that while I am studying *Hamlet* I come across a word with two meanings which seems ironic. Before Hamlet knows about his father being murdered, he is already disgusted at the indecent haste of his mother's marriage to Claudius. Hamlet continues to wear black, but Gertrude urges him to forget his father's death, using the argument that everybody has to die in the end. In the second scene I find this exchange between them:

> GERTRUDE.   Thou know'st 'tis common – all that lives must die,
> Passing through nature to eternity.
> HAMLET.   Ay, madam, it is common.
>   (*Hamlet*, I.ii.72-4, *The Complete Works*, Collins, 1964)

The word 'common' means one thing to Gertrude, but Hamlet seems to suggest another meaning.

Before I can comment on this I must define the two meanings of 'common' as Hamlet and Gertrude use it. Gertrude uses the word in the sense of 'usual', and asks Hamlet to behave in the 'usual' way by overcoming his grief. She is only talking about his father's death. Hamlet uses 'common' in its other sense, meaning 'vulgar' or 'disgusting'. He is referring to his father's death, but he is also commenting on her, her new husband, her over-quick marriage, and on the behaviour she expects from him. I have found a word with two meanings, then, and I have defined what the two meanings are. So far I know that 'common' is a pun; it is not necessarily ironic. The definition of irony says that both the meanings must be valid in the text, and there must be a relationship between them, so before I know whether 'common' is ironic I have more to do. The question is, do the two meanings of 'common' represent different attitudes which are significant in the text as a whole? In other words, is there more behind 'common' than just a pun?

It might seem difficult to relate two meanings of a word or sentence to the text as a whole, because it is difficult to think about the text as a whole. In this situation, go for the obvious: in our example the two meanings of 'common' are expressed by two characters, so the clearest way to relate them to bigger elements of the text is to think about the characters involved. Think about the relationship between each meaning, and the theme or character it relates to. Here are notes on the two meanings of 'common' in relation to Gertrude's and Hamlet's characters.

Gertrude's meaning. Gertrude will live as most people do, eating, drinking, making love, and forgetting about death. She will not think carefully about right and wrong, or virtue. She will do what is 'common' or 'usual', and be contented.

Hamlet's meaning. Hamlet, on the other hand, finds 'common' life disgusting. He seeks something pure, and is unable to forget about death, sin and judgement. Hamlet admired his father, and he finds it disgusting that his mother can overcome her grief so quickly, or at all. Elsewhere in the play we see that Hamlet tries to stamp out 'common' feelings in himself. He loves the beautiful Ophelia, but hates the lustful feelings she arouses in him. He abuses her roughly and tells her to stop arousing these 'common' animal feelings in him by going away to live in a nunnery.

The two meanings of 'common', then, reflect the different attitudes of the two characters. Hamlet's feeling of disgust at humanity, and Gertrude's comfortable immorality. I have established, therefore, that both the meanings are significant in the text. When you know that the meanings you have come across are part of a larger complexity in the text, examine them as a paradox: they are different and they contradict each other, but do they both have some truth in them? Look at the argument between Hamlet and Gertrude. In what senses are both right? First, Gertrude is right: you cannot mourn for ever, life must go on because you must eat, drink and laugh, and there is a kingdom to rule. Death is 'common' and you have to forget about it in order to live. On the other hand, Hamlet is also right: Gertrude has married too quickly, and forgotten his father too willingly. People are 'common' because they pursue their own desires without regard to moral principles, and without thinking about death and judgement. They are both right, yet they contradict each other, so the relationship between the two meanings of 'common' is a paradox.

I now know that the pun on 'common' is ironic. Notice the stages I have gone through in order to establish and understand irony:

(i)   Define the different meanings you notice in the text.
(ii) Choose a theme or characters which are likely to relate to these meanings, and describe how the meanings represent larger elements in the characters or themes of the text.

(iii) When you know that the two meanings are significant, explain how the two together make a paradox by being contradictory, and at the same time both valid. When you have completed these stages you understand the relationships between different elements of the text, because you have explored the paradoxical or ironic complexity of the world of the text.

Now you can think about the world of the text as a whole, and see whether the irony you have analysed has broader implications: does your irony relate to more than the one theme or characters you have chosen to focus on? Thinking about *Hamlet* I can understand that the paradox of 'common' represents a central tragic irony in the play: we admire Hamlet for his honesty and intellect, and he claims our sympathy, but at the same time we know that the world cannot be ruled by men like him. The 'common' king, Claudius the murderer, is a good politician and in many ways a good king. The irony I first noticed in one word, then, is found to represent different attitudes in different characters, and finally is a paradoxical double truth which is central to the meaning of the play as a whole. In other words, the further you investigate an ironic paradox, the more its significance in the text grows. This is a peculiar effect of irony which will help you to recognise it. Understanding the paradoxical relationship between different parts of the text gives a feeling of satisfaction. Here, we understand how two attitudes, which are in conflict throughout the play, can both be right at the same time. We understand this quickly because two important attitudes are suddenly represented in one word. The irony gives a feeling of sudden insight and wholeness, as if you suddenly understand the text from a new, full perspective.

I have tried to show you how irony can be studied in detail, using the example from *Hamlet*, and how irony is a point of view, a way of presenting the complexity of things. Irony of this kind can be found in a great many works of literature, because it is a way of suggesting the complexity of a situation, character, or event. Irony always suggests that there is no single truth which can be stated in a direct way: there is often more than one way of looking at things, and contradictory meanings can be equally valid. Discussing irony in a text, which can be as straightforward as focusing on one word, as in our example from *Hamlet*, is therefore an especially rewarding approach. It is so because you focus on a very small effect in the text, yet this small effect reveals strikingly the kind of complex statement about experience that a whole text can make.

You do not, however, find irony only in words or sentences with two meanings. The rest of this chapter explains two other ways in which the ironic insight is revealed. There is no need to go over the method in detail again, but some brief examples of these other forms of irony will help you to identify the ironic effect. Irony is a new point of view on the text. You gain new understanding of the text when something unexpected happens, or when a secret is revealed. When you have read a text, it is worthwhile to think about it as a whole and pay particular attention to unexpected events and surprising revelations. The ironical insight may come suddenly as a surprise is revealed; at other times irony only penetrates gently and gradually as you think about the text. Jane Austen's novels show clear examples of both these effects. Here are accounts of each kind drawn from *Emma* and *Pride and Prejudice.*

Towards the end of *Emma* we discover that two of the main characters, Jane Fairfax and Frank Churchill, have been secretly engaged all through the novel. This revelation puts two versions of the truth together suddenly: Jane and Frank have no particualr relationship (as they have pretended all along); Jane and Frank are in love and engaged to be married (which is suddenly revealed at the end). The effect of suddenly comparing this revelation with all the events we have already read about is to make us reinterpret everything these two characters have said and done in the novel from a new point of view. A new ironical light is cast over the whole text, and we realise how two-sided the world of the novel is: the two versions of the truth were there all along, but our new knowledge gives a new interpretation to old events. The surprising revelation of their relationship, then, floods the whole text with a new ironic light of understanding. The effect, typical of irony, is to make us feel that we understand the complexity of life. Life is not as simple as we thought: it is a complex reality, ironically capable of two paradoxical interpretations.

A gentler irony is part of the effect of *Pride and Prejudice*, the novel I discussed in Chapter 2. This time the ironical understanding penetrates gradually as we study the text in detail and become increasingly familiar with what it is about and what eventually happens in the story. Here is the first sentence of *Pride and Prejudice*:

It is a truth universally acknowledged, that a single man in possession of a good fortune must be in want of a wife.

(*Pride and Prejudice*, Penguin, 1972, p. 51)

You must laugh at this sentence the first time you read it because it seems to be sarcastic. It ridicules an over-simplified idea of marriage, and Jane Austen and the reader join together in laughing. We are too intelligent to think that every well-off single man is looking for a wife, rather as if he were going shopping. When you have finished reading the novel, sit and reflect about what actually happens. The 'single man in possession of a good fortune' is a character called Mr Bingley. The absurd idea that he must be looking for a wife belongs to a character called Mrs Bennet. She is convinced that Mr Bingley is exactly the kind of young man who must marry somebody, and to your surprise you realise that Mrs Bennet's idea comes true. Mr Bingley marries her daughter Jane Bennet at the end of the book. The ridiculous idea you laughed at turns out to be right after all! The first sentence seemed to be sarcastic, then, so you rejected the ludicrous meaning (marriage is like going shopping). The outcome of the text as a whole ironically revives that meaning and gives a new ironical insight into the events and characters throughout. The new insight is a paradox: you were right to laugh at the silly attitude to marriage expressed in the first sentence, yet events show that the absurd view is often ironically right. Irony again casts a new light over significant elements of the text as a whole. Romantic and commercial attitudes to marriage are a theme of *Pride and Prejudice*. The reader sympathises with the more romantic attitude of Elizabeth Bennet, stressing the importance of love, kindness, and other human emotional qualities rather than money and social position. The outcome laughs at you for being so idealistic. After all, the romantic heroine Elizabeth marries a very rich man in the end.

The two examples I have just explained raise a further point. Several people are part of a literary text: characters, the reader, the author. Jane Austen knew more about what would happen than the reader was allowed to know. You can say then, that the irony of Frank's and Jane's secret engagement in *Emma* is a matter of the difference between the author's knowledge and the reader's ignorance. Any difference between what one person knows and what another knows can produce irony: some characters know more than others, the reader or audience often knows more than the characters. This effect is called **dramatic irony**. A common example occurs in pantomime where the villain stands behind the hero and tries to kill him. The hero asks the audience what is wrong, unaware of the villain's presence. Children in the audience are roused to screaming excitement by the ironic difference between what they know and the hero's ignorance.

Most literary texts use this device, often in extended fashion, as in this next example. In the play *The School for Scandal* by R. B. Sheridan, Charles Surface expects to inherit his rich Uncle Oliver's fortune. In the meantime he arranges to borrow money from a money-lender called Mr Premium. Uncle Oliver pretends to be Mr Premium and comes to arrange the loan. He asks Charles about his financial prospects. The extract below shows how much amusement Sheridan makes out of the ironic situation. The audience knows, but Charles does not know, that he is really talking to his uncle about his uncle. Charles suggests that he will repay the loan when Sir Oliver dies:

CHARLES S. Though at the same time the old fellow has been so liberal to me, that I give you my word I should be very sorry to hear that anything had happened to him.

SIR OLIVER S. Not more than *I* should, I assure you. But the bond you mention happens to be just the worst security you could offer me – for I might live to a hundred and never recover the principal.

CHARLES S. Oh, yes, you would – the moment Sir Oliver dies, you know you would come on me for the money.

SIR OLIVER S. Then I believe I should be the most unwelcome dun you ever had in you life.

CHARLES S. What! I suppose you are afraid now that Sir Oliver is too good a life?

SIR OLIVER S. No, indeed, I am not; though I have heard he is as hale and healthy as any man of his years in Christendom.

CHARLES S. There again you are misinformed. No, no, the climate has hurt him considerably, poor Uncle Oliver! Yes, he breaks apace, I'm told – and is so much altered lately, that his nearest relations don't know him.

SIR OLIVER S. No! ha! ha! ha! so much altered lately, that his nearest relations don't know him! – that's droll, egad – ha! ha! ha!

CHARLES S. Ha! ha! – you're glad to hear that, little Premium?

SIR OLIVER S. No, no, I'm not.

(*School for Scandal*, ULP, 1967, Act III, scene iii, 163-85)

The difference Sheridan exploits is between what the audience and Sir Oliver know, and what Charles does not know. This enables Sir Oliver to speak with deliberate double meanings, while Charles speaks with unconscious double meanings, and the writer gets the most amusement out of the complexity of knowledge and ignorance.

The examples I have described should help you to find and think about irony. The definition at the beginning of this chapter said that irony exists where two or more meanings can be understood from what is written. The clearest way to find two meanings in a text is to look for words or sentences which have two meanings. That is how I found irony in *Hamlet*. Now add two other ways of discovering irony: first, think about surprise events and revelations in the text you are studying. Surprises change the way you think about the text, so they create a second 'meaning' or 'attitude' to the text which gives rise to irony. Second, find differences between what the different people in the text know. If any one of author, characters or readers knows more than another, dramatic irony is produced. The definition said that irony arises from two different 'meanings'. 'Meanings' has to be understood in its broadest sense. Look for two or more meanings, attitudes, understandings, points of view, amounts of knowledge: all these can produce irony.

HOW TO DESCRIBE IRONY

I have explained what irony is, how to find it and how to study it. The aim of studying irony, however, is to describe the feeling it conveys to the reader. Understanding irony tells you how the writer creates an effect. To understand the text, describe the feeling irony produces. For example, the hopeless paradox of Hamlet's and Gertrude's attitudes to life is a tragic irony because it makes us understand that the best man cannot succeed in life: Hamlet is doomed by his own pure nature. Jane Austen's laughing comment on marriage is a cynical irony because it reminds us that even lovers have to eat and pay the rent. Sheridan's dramatic irony is amusing and shows us what fools people make of themselves when they do not know what is happening. The adjectives I have used to describe the ironies discussed as examples in this chapter are ordinary words which describe feelings and states of mind: tragic, cynical, amusing. Irony produces a range of different feelings, sometimes funny and sometimes bitter or even frightening. Use ordinary adjectives to describe the feeling or state of mind that the irony you have analysed produces.

In this chapter the examples have shown quite a lot about the effect irony produces. Here are some of the main points. Irony adds to or changes our understanding of the text. This may be because something unexpected happens which we realise is true, or which we should have expected, or because we understand the paradoxical relationship between different kinds of truth, between the different meanings and attitudes which make up the complex reality of the text. Because irony increases our understanding, its effect is satisfying. We often notice irony suddenly in a word or a sentence, or a sudden event which reveals a new truth; yet irony changes and increases our understanding of a whole work. Because irony is a brief moment of realisation which changes everything, it can give intense satisfaction as if we are suddenly flooded with understanding.

Irony introduces an extra, ironical point of view, with which we look anew at all the other attitudes in the text. From the ironical point of view we understand the complexity of experience which the writer seeks to convey. Literature is about different elements and attitudes which are contradictory but all, in different ways, true or valid. Different points of view which are all to some extent true are called paradoxes. Irony helps you to understand the paradoxical nature of reality. Understanding irony is therefore an incalculable help in understanding what literature is about, and in understanding its complexity.

CONCLUSION

Perhaps the best final piece of advice I can give about irony is to use the word very carefully. Let me explain the reason for this: every chapter of this book has stressed the idea that literature presents an impression of the complexity of life. In each chapter I have shown that you can concentrate on various aspects of a text to develop your sense of its complexity. Nowhere is this link between study and complexity more direct than in the writer's use of irony. It is a way of writing which powerfully presents the complex, contradictory, multi-faceted nature of life. Students who have realised this, however, sometimes fall into an almost automatic response of saying how ironic everything about the text is. This is why I advise you to use the word irony carefully, ensuring that you only comment on irony when you are analysing a specific example and showing how the text actually operates.

This caution is consistent with everything I have said during the course of this book. Indeed, by this stage I feel that my central advice can be expressed in just two points. The first is that the aim of study is to capture and convey something of the complexity of a literary text.

The second point is that the only way to do this is to look at the text itself, the most rewarding approach being to focus on significant short passages. Even when you have developed your view of a text, however, there is always another stage. You will want to or have to write about the texts you study, and most of this writing will be in the form of essays. Writing essays can be a chore, but, as the next two chapters explain, if you go about it logically and see what you are asked to do, essays can soon become satisfying end products from all your studying, and you will be able to tackle them with confidence.

6

Writing an essay I

THE LITERATURE EXAMINATION

THE aim of studying literature is to gain an understanding of your texts, of how and why they were written, but the practical question of how to write in the examination so that you do justice to your understanding and pass with a good grade is an important problem for most students. Although several different forms of examination are set for literature, your main task in any of them will be writing essays, so these two chapters focus on how to write essays about the texts you have studied. You will probably be asked to write essays both as part of your course and in the examination at the end. I will be discussing what to do in the examination, but the essays you write at home are much the same, you just have more time to write them. The advice I give, though based on examinations, applies to all the essays you write.

Essays have to be planned and organised to suit the particular question you are answering, the text you are writing about and the views you want to put forward. It follows that there is no single formula which will make an ideal essay for every situation. The important point is to understand what you are doing and what you are expected to do when you write an essay. I have divided the two most important points to grasp into these two chapters. This one is about thinking, and planning your essay so that it answers the question. I shall say something about writing the first and last paragraphs as we go along, but this chapter is mainly about the logical thinking which ensures that you write an organised and relevant essay. The next chapter deals with writing about texts and shows how to write so you make points about the text strongly, and develop your critical ideas. This chapter, then, is about thinking and the next is about writing. If you read these two chapters, a bit of practice will enable you to tackle any question on your texts confidently, and you may even find that the chore of essay-writing turns into a satisfying pleasure because you know you are writing well.

Like other exams, the literature paper tests your knowledge and learning of facts. Unlike many other exams, however, literature questions test you in many other ways as well. I have emphasised that each text you study is a complex world, and the examination tests your understanding and your response to this complex living world. The qualities which make you a thoughtful and sensitive person are being tested: your independence, judgement, sensitivity, confidence, not to mention how well you can think under pressure. The literature paper, then, is unlike many other exams because it tests your maturity as a person.

THE ESSAY QUESTION

Literature questions often seem casual. In History you are told to 'state' the reasons for the outbreak of World War I, in Biology you are asked directly 'what is' an amoeba, in various subjects you have to 'solve' this or 'calculate' that. The literature examiner uses gentler language. 'Consider', he suggests, 'discuss', or 'how far do you agree that', or 'what are your views on', he politely asks. The language of literature questions is more human because, as I have explained, they test your human qualities as well as your knowledge. You must not confuse this polite language of the questions with casualness, however. The questions are not casual at all. Imagine the question is a prescription and you are a chemist. When the doctor writes a prescription, he relies on the chemist to mix the right ingredients in the right proportions to make the right medicine. The chemist must read the prescription carefully, and put the right things into the medicine, otherwise the patient might die. It is the same with literature questions: read them carefully and put the right things in your answer, and the medicine will be right. In this chapter I take these two tasks in turn, first explaining how to analyse the question; then showing how to make sure you put the right things into your answer.

Before tackling these two points, however, there is a possible confusion to get out of the way. Do you have any freedom in how you answer the question, or is there only one 'right' answer? Can you disagree with the question? This confusion arises because literature is complex and alive, not cut and dried like Mathematics. In studying a text you have thought about it, analysed it, and developed your ideas based on your own response. Your understanding of the text is not quite the same as anyone else's: it is your own understanding which reflects your feelings and emphasises the parts of the text which seem particularly important to you. So you have some freedom: you can express your own point of view, disagreeing with the opinions put forward in the question. Your only master is the text, because everything you write about it must be supported by evidence, and reasonably drawn from what the author wrote and what happens in the story. You are free to disagree with the question, then, but you must support your views from the text.

This freedom must not be confused with an entirely different matter. You cannot disobey the examiner. He has total power over you, and you must carry out the orders he gives. Do not write about anything the examiner does not tell you to write about, just write an answer which fits the question. This brings us back to filling the examiner's prescription: analyse the question carefully, and put the right things into your answer.

Analyse the question

A literature question asks you to consider one part or some parts of the world of the text. It may ask about a character or a theme, or ask you to explain the significance of one important event or episode. Questions can be quite complicated, however, so your first job is to define which aspect of the text the question is about. Do this by noticing the important words and phrases in the question. Any words or phrases which stand for part of the world of the text, or raise a controversial point about the text, tell you what your essay must be about. If you just read the question once, think you understand it, and immediately plunge into writing, you are likely to go wrong. You will not notice or you will forget part of the subject it asks you about . For this reason you must not take any short cuts, but analyse the question carefully. Here is a question on Shakespeare's *The Winter's Tale*, which I'm going to use as an example of how to analyse questions and plan essays:

Consider the view that in *The Winter's Tale* Shakespeare compares the sophistication of the court with the simplicity of the country and draws a clear moral lesson from this contrast.

First, underline important and controversial words and phrases in the question, so you define the part of the text your question asks about. In this case I underline sophistication of the court, simplicity of the country, draws a clear moral lesson and contrast. Each of these words and phrases from the question poses a question for me to discuss and answer, so each of these four parts of the question can be rewritten as a subquestion in its own right. When you have underlined the important words and phrases, then, turn them into questions. This makes the subject of your essay clear by defining exactly what points you have to decide. My question on *The Winter's Tale* can be turned into four subquestions, as follows:

1. Do the court scenes show sophistication?
2. Do the country scenes show simplicity?
3. Does Shakespeare draw a clear moral lesson from comparing court and country?
4. Do court and country contrast?

The important words and phrases from the question are the ingredients in the medicine I have to prepare. By making a thorough list of them in analysing the question, you can ensure that you are dealing with the question thoroughly and clearly.

Now I have analysed the question. There are four topics I must deal with in my essay. The next stage is to make sure that they are put into the most sensible and logical order. The argument you put forward in your essay should develop logically, so it is important to work out how the different topics follow each other and lead to a conclusion. In this case I begin by describing the court and the country, because I cannot say much about them, or know whether they contrast, until I have explained what they are like. As soon as I have described them, however, I can discuss whether they contrast. Only then, when I have dealt with the other three topics, can I begin to look for any moral lesson which may come from a contrast I may or may not have found between the court and the country. The plan for my essay, therefore, looks like this:

1. The court (sophistication?)
2. The country (simplicity?)
3. Is there a contrast?
4. Does Shakespeare draw a clear moral lesson from this contrast?

Notice that the essay-plan I have written deals with all the important words and phrases I underlined in the question, but I have changed their order to fit the only logical and sensible way I can discuss them.

When you have found the important words and phrases from the question, turned them into subquestions or topics, and put them into logical order, you have written a plan for your essay. If you then write thoroughly about the list of topics in your plan, you will be putting the right things into your essay. At this stage you are ready to write the opening paragraph of your essay. The opening paragraph should be a prospectus of what you intend to write, a kind of promise, or 'contents page', for the essay. Here is the opening paragraph I would write for my essay on *The Winter's Tale*:

In examining this view of *The Winter's Tale* I shall look closely at the way Shakespeare portrays the court and the country in the play, so I can define the contrast between them. Then I shall discuss whether Shakespeare uses this contrast to put forward a moral lesson about simplicity and sophistication.

This opening paragraph is nothing more than the essay-plan written out in sentences. It lists the topics the essay will discuss, in the order in which they will be discussed. Notice that the first paragraph you write must be brief and to the point. In an exam you have no time to spare, so it is important to get straight down to answering the question like this. Do not write any elaborate introduction, or give any background information; the question does not ask you to do that. All you have been told to do is answer the question, and that is all you have time for. With some practice, and depending on the complexity of the question, you can be finishing your first paragraph after two or three minutes from the start. There is a further step to take, however, before you are ready to write the rest of the essay. I have explained how to analyse the question by defining the different topics it prescribes. When you have done this, it is important to define the parts of the text you will use as evidence when you write about each topic. Always analyse the question before you choose what you will refer to in your answer: the right time to choose your quotations and references is then.

When the text is a collection of poems, the question usually asks you to choose poems to refer to in your answer. You can only make an appropriate choice after you have analysed the question. If, for example, you have studied the poems of W. B. Yeats, you might face this question:

Discuss Yeats's use of symbolism, using either **two** or **three** examples from his works.

Analysing the question is straightforward. Underline Yeats's use of sym-bolism; you do not need to worry about an order of topics because that is the only topic prescribed in the question. Choosing two or three poems is more difficult, because you must choose poems which contain examples of symbolism. With such a question many students rush in and begin writing about their three favourite poems, but that is not what is required. Always choose your material after analysing the question; then you will choose the right material for the topics the question prescribes. In this case, choose three symbolic poems, not necessarily your three favourite poems. Many essay-questions are like this, seeming to offer unlimited choice, but when you define the question and define the material you will use in your answer, you discover that the choice is quite limited after all: you can only use material which is directly rele-vant to the topics in the question.

This question about Yeats's poetry raises another matter. Analys-ing the question was easy, but I am still left with a big, difficult critical term: 'symbolism'. If I am not careful I might go ahead and write the essay with a vague and rather woolly idea of what symbolism is, so the essay will be loose and will lack direction. The important thing for me to do at the outset is to define 'symbolism' clearly, so I can relate the examples I use from Yeats's poems to a clear and defined idea of what symbolism is. This helps to discipline the rest of my essay: it would ensure that I did look at symbols, not just at the three poems in general, and that I did really discuss how Yeats uses symbols. This advice applies whenever a fairly difficult term, such as 'tragedy', 'comedy', 'realism' or 'allegory' appears in a question. Use the first paragraph to analyse the question, as I have already shown; but also in the first paragraph, define the words which are key difficult terms in the question, so you know how you will discuss them. Then you can select your examples and quotations.

You will often find that the quotations and references you choose define themselves. Most texts have vital or outstanding passages, which you know well by the time you have studied for the exam. Certain important topics in the text cannot be properly discussed without referring to these important passages, so the examiner will expect you to discuss them in your essay. For example, in Shakespeare's *Hamlet*, Hamlet considers suicide. If you were answering a question on this theme of suicide in the play, you would have to refer to those soliloquies where Hamlet contemplates suicide and sets out his attitude to death. The examiner expects to find these speeches referred to in your essay, because you could not answer the question properly if you ignored them.

Having chosen your quotations you are ready to write the essay itself. There might seem a lot of work to do before you reach this stage, but really it amounts to no more than three simple moves: analyse the question, write your first paragraph, then choose the bits of the text you are going to refer to at each stage of your essay. The main thing is that you have done the thinking first: you have a list of topics which you can rely on and use as a checklist, referring to the plan and ticking off the topics as you deal with them. Now you can concentrate on how you write about the text. You have done the thinking, so you should not have to stop and wonder where you are or what comes next in the middle of writing the essay. I will be talking about how to write the essay in the next chapter, but first I want to say something about how to write your last paragraph, because writing a conclusion brings us back to the thinking part of essay-work again.

Answer the question

If you use your plan as a checklist, you are sure to work through the subject-matter of the essay in the same logical order you have worked out while analysing the question, so you are sure to cover all aspects of the question thoroughly. In an examination you will be nervous and rushed. This method prevents you from losing your head and missing out parts of the subject, so the next problem you face comes when you have dealt with all the topics on your list. When you have discussed each topic on your plan, how do you write a conclusion?

A conclusion, of course, is a chance to sum up all the analysis and discussion you have written in the main body of your essay, and you should use it to make a final statement on where your developing ideas have led you to in the end. In this sense you write a conclusion to your essay. It is important to remember, however, that at the same time you are meant to be answering the question. This is sometimes difficult because writing the essay has filled your mind with the variety and complexity of the text: concentrating on quotations, analysing in detail and developing your ideas, you might have forgotten about the question you are answering. To make sure your conclusion is relevant, stop before you write it, and look back to the original question. The knack is to imagine you are face to face with the examiner, and the question and answer are part of a conversation between you. Forget the desk, paper, pens, and all the paraphernalia of the examination. Think only this: somebody has asked me a question, which I will now answer.

Suppose, for example, I am writing an essay to answer this question on Jane Austen's *Pride and Prejudice*:

How far do you agree that Elizabeth learns to curb her high spirits, while her sister Jane learns that she must show her feelings more openly?

Students sometimes think that a conclusion has to sound fine, grand and final, so they write a vague generalisation about what an enduring comic masterpiece *Pride and Prejudice* is, and how generations of readers have enjoyed Jane Austen's ironic brilliance. The question, of course, did not ask anything about that. The examiner asked about Jane and Elizabeth, so a big generalisation does not answer the question. Again, in the nervous tension of an examination you might write a conclusion which answers about Elizabeth, but forget the other part which was about Jane. The examiner can only give half-marks to an answer about one sister, because he asked about both of them. Stop to reread the question, then, before you write your conclusion. This helps to make sure that your answer is both relevant and thorough. Here is the concluding paragraph I would write at the end of my essay on *Pride and Prejudice*. Notice that I use the conclusion both to sum up the views I have developed about the two sisters in the main body of my essay, and in the end to give a direct answer to the question I was asked:

Elizabeth seems more restrained at the end of the novel, but the final chapter suggests that she will soon become playful again and so her more sober manners are not likely to be lasting. Jane suffers from her quiet manner, appearing so calm that neither Bingley nor Darcy could detect her love. However, she wins Bingley in the end thanks to Elizabeth and Darcy's encouragement of the courtship, not through any change in manner. In conclusion, then, I would say that Elizabeth does learn to control her high spirits, although this does not represent a permanent change in her character, while Jane does not change her manner at all or show her feelings more openly at any time during the novel.

Notice that my discussion of the two characters has led to a thorough direct answer, and the answer I give about Elizabeth is different from the one I give about Jane, because that is what I have found from analysing them both. I have filled the examiner's prescription, then, by putting the right ingredients into my answer, but I have disagreed with the view put forward in the question. Another candidate might give a different answer, disagreeing with a different part of the question, or disagreeing with what I think. This underlines what I said earlier about your freedom: you can disagree about the text as long as you have evidence and your argument is reasonable, but you cannot disobey the question in what it tells you to discuss.

CONCLUSION

The thinking part of essay-work keeps your essays disciplined, relevant, and makes sure that your answer develops in a sensible logical order. If you do the thinking work methodically before you start to write, this sets you free to concentrate properly on how you write and on the complexity of the text while you are writing the main part of your essay. Really, essay-writing should follow a sequence similar to the three steps I have been using for studying literature in this book: begin by thinking and making the important logical decisions which will act as a guide as you work on, then work in detail on the close analysis of the text, and finally relate your ideas together to reach a broad understanding which acts as a conclusion, leading to a direct answer to the original question.

7

Writing an essay II

MAKING A CASE

THIS chapter is about how to write the main part of your essay, that is the paragraphs which are about the text and which come in between the introductory paragraph and the conclusion. When you study literature you develop a complex response to the complex world of the text. Your feelings are enlisted as you read, so you have a personal relationship with the text. A personal relationship is not a matter of 'facts', because feelings and experiences cannot be measured or counted. It follows that there is no single 'right' answer to a literature question. Your views on the text are not ticked and crossed like your answers in Mathematics. Instead of 'right' or 'wrong', different adjectives describe good and bad literature essays: they are 'reasonable', 'convincing' and 'persuasive', or they are 'ridiculous' 'irrelevant' or 'unsupported'. Your task when you write an essay is to be reasonable, convincing and persuasive in explaining your point of view. You hope the examiner will be convinced that your views are reasonable, so your ideas have to be *proved beyond reasonable doubt.*

The phrase in italics comes from the language of a courtroom. I use a legal phrase because writing a literature essay is very like what a lawyer does in court. The lawyer must prove his case beyond reasonable doubt to convince the judge and jury that his version of what happened is the true one. He has to argue logically and make good use of all the evidence. This comparison between essay-writing and a court of law is very useful because it explains how important evidence is in your essays. It also explains what you are trying to do in an essay, and that is to present a solid argument, a solid case in which you support your views with logical reasoning and evidence. When you write an essay, then, use evidence in the same way a lawyer does. Marshal good evidence which supports your view of the text, and explain what the

102

evidence shows, linking each point with reasoned discussion and argument. Your aim is to convince the examiner that your view is more likely to be the truth than any other. If you write an essay without any evidence from the text, the examiner will not be convinced that you really know what you are talking about and certainly will not be persuaded by your answer.

HOW TO WRITE A SIMPLE PARAGRAPH

As I remarked in the last chapter, there are so many different essay-questions and texts you might face that no simple formula for writing essays will work for all of them. I am not going to tell you, therefore, how many paragraphs to put in your essays, or give elaborate advice about how to write linking-pieces between one point and the next. The organised thinking I wrote about in the last chapter, with a bit of practice, will take care of the overall shape and development of your argument and ideas, and you will add polish to your style with more practice. The main point to concentrate on now is how to write a paragraph, in particular on how to make a point about a literary text so that it is secure and convincing.

The paragraph is the basic unit of your essay. It deals with one subject, and if you learn to write good clear paragraphs you can simply string them together in order, covering the topics in your plan, and the result will be an essay. A simple paragraph is one which sets out to make one statement about the text. More complicated paragraphs may discuss a whole topic or aspect of the text, but they are all based on the first need to make one statement securely and convincingly.

Whenever you make a statement about the text, you must give your evidence for making that statement, and explain how the evidence supports the statement. Here is a statement about Elizabeth Bennet in *Pride and Prejudice*:

Elizabeth has lively and playful manners.

This is a very simple statement about her, but anybody can disagree with it. It is just an assertion, so another reader could say Elizabeth is quiet and dull, and I cannot argue because I have only said what I think without giving any reason why I happen to think that way. This statement, then, is vulnerable because anyone can say I am wrong. It is open to attack because it is not supported by evidence. To make my statement more secure and persuasive I must now point to the evidence of the text: Elizabeth has lively and playful manners. She tells her friends about Darcy's refusal to dance with her with great spirit, because, as Jane Austen remarks, she 'had a lively, playful disposition, which delighted in anything ridiculous'.

Any reader who wants to disagree with me now has to attack the quotation, which shows clearly that Elizabeth has a lively and playful disposition. My statement about the text is therefore secure: it is difficult to contradict, and it is convincing because I have put forward evidence which supports it. The rule to follow when you write about literature, then, is that all your statements about the text must be supported by evidence.

The evidence in my example from *Pride and Prejudice* is a quotation from the text. A reference to the text is also evidence. Use references when you make a statement about the events of the story, or when a quotation would be too long and clumsy because your statement describes a whole conversation or a long passage. Here is a statement about one of the episodes in Wilkie Collins's novel *The Woman in White*, together with the reference which provides the evidence to support it. You do not need to know the novel to see how this reference works, only that in the episode I am referring to one of the main characters manages to overhear the villains when they are making their wicked plans:

Wilkie Collins heightens suspense in the scene where Marian eavesdrops on the Count and Sir Percival, by putting her in the most uncomfortable and dangerous position (**statement**). She is on a ledge so narrow she cannot straighten her feet, a row of flowerpots is on the outer edge, ready to fall and give her away, she is nearly beneath Madame Fosco's window, and it is raining hard (**evidence**).

The evidence which shows that Marian was in an uncomfortable and dangerous position is made up of a number of points which are drawn from the description of the whole episode in the text. The episode spans about twenty printed pages, and gives a lot of other details as well, both about the layout and design of the house where it takes place, and the villains' conversation. These things are not relevant to the statement, which is only about Marian's dangerous position, so a quotation would be hopelessly lengthy and clumsy. I have simply selected the relevant points to support my statement, and referred to them. When a quotation would be clumsy or unnecessary, then, refer to the evidence which supports your statement as I have done in the example above.

The evidence in a literature essay is the text you have studied. Use the text as quotations or references to support your statements. This makes your statements secure, rather than vulnerable. Remember that quotations from critics or study-aids are not evidence. They should never appear in your essays. The examiner is interested in your understanding of the text, and how you have developed your ideas from direct study of the text. He is not interested in what other people think. You may, of course, have read some critics, and you may have found that their way of looking at the text has helped you to understand some things better. The argument you put forward in your essay, however, has to be reasonable in its own right: it must be based on the text, and you should not refer to any other supposed 'authority'.

In building up our simple paragraph, we have written a statement and added the evidence which supports it. This on its own, however, is not enough: literature is complex, and you have studied the text closely, developing a sense of complexity and analysing with precision and in detail. A simple statement will not do justice to the complex understanding you have, nor will it adequately represent the subtlety of the text. When you have made your statement and added the evidence, then, the rest of your paragraph has to show more precision and complex detail, developing your initial idea. To develop your point, making your first simple statement more accurate and complex, either ask the question 'Why?' or compare the statement with the evidence. I can show how these different methods work by two examples.

First, here is a statement I made about the style of Gerard Manley Hopkins's 'The Wreck of the *Deutschland*', in Chapter 4. I have put evidence with it which supports the statement:

Hopkins's language is extemely violent, full of physical strain with overtones of pain and punishment (**statement**). For example, the words 'lashed', 'rod', 'sweep', 'hurl' and 'trod' all occur within seven lines in stanza two (**evidence**).

I have made a secure statement about the text. Now I can ask the question 'Why', I can ask what purpose is served by such a violent and physical style. I have explained how the text is, but I can develop my point by thinking about why the text is like that. Here is my answer to the question 'Why does Hopkins use so many violent physical words?', which completes my paragraph:

The subject of the stanza itself is spiritual experience; so it seems that Hopkins uses violent physical language to make his spiritual experience more vivid and real to us, to convey his religious feelings more directly to the reader (**developing the idea** by asking the question 'Why').

The other way to develop the idea of a paragraph is to compare your statement and the evidence. You will often find yourself making a straightforward statement about the text at the start of a paragraph, then using evidence which is more detailed than the simple point it illustrates. When this happens, write a more detailed discussion of the evidence as the last part of the paragraph. This develops your idea by making it more complex and precise. A clear example comes from *Huckleberry Finn* by Mark Twain. Suppose I want to say that Huck, the main character, is a kind and sympathetic character. That is a simple statement about Huck. I decide to use a quotation which shows that Huck is shocked and touched when he sees two men tarred and feathered by the people of a Mississippi town. The cruelty of their punishment touches Huck's heart, so the quotation offers solid evidence to support the statement that he is kind and sympathetic. When I think about this quotation and compare it to my simple statement, however, I can see there is much more to it than just soft-heartedness. The two men Huck is sorry for are his enemies, they have previously robbed him and sold his best friend into slavery. So the quotation shows more than Huck's soft heart, it shows that he can feel sympathy even for his enemies, and that he abhors cruelty even when its victims deserve it. I can, then, use this idea to develop my paragraph, drawing on the quotation to make a further point about Huck after the main simple statement has been established.

Huck is soft-hearted and feels sympathy for other people (**statement**). We see this when he witnesses the cruel punishment of the King and the Duke, and says: 'I was sorry for them poor pitiful rascals, it seemed like I couldn't ever feel any hardness against them any more in the world' (**evidence**). The fact that Huck feels this way about the King and the Duke, who have previously robbed and betrayed him and sold his best friend into slavery, shows that Huck is more than soft-hearted:

he forgives people quickly, and hates to see cruelty or suffering whether the punishment is deserved or not (**developing the idea** by comparing statement and evidence).

These two paragraphs I have written as examples, one about 'The Wreck of the *Deutschland*' and the other on *Huckleberry Finn*, are complete paragraphs for essays. They contain three elements: a statement about the text, evidence which supports the statement, and development of the idea either by asking the question 'Why?' or by comparing statement and evidence. These three elements are the basic material of literature essays, and should normally come in the order I have shown. The examples above are only simple paragraphs, which set out to make one statement about the text. Essay-questions, however, often require you to make more complex statements about a text. You might have to compare two ideas or two characters, for example. The next section shows how to use the same three basic elements I have described here to build more complicated paragraphs, so you can cope with the requirements of any question and write convincing, well-supported essays.

HOW TO WRITE MORE COMPLICATED PARAGRAPHS

Many of the paragraphs you write will be more complicated than the simple examples in the last section, because you will be dealing with complexities of the text or complexities in the question. The kind of paragraph I have explained is, however, the basic unit for essays. The combination of statement, evidence and development of the idea makes your views on the text secure, and develops your first statements so they become more subtle and accurate. When the statement you are making is more complex, perhaps because the question makes you consider two points of view at once, then your paragraph will also become more complicated. For example, any paragraph which brings out a contrast in the text will need more of the elements I have described: you might find it best to make two statements, or you might need to bring forward two quotations as evidence. Finally you might develop your ideas in stages, perhaps separately first before you bring them together at the end of the paragraph.

Building more elements into a paragraph is not so difficult, however. The basic structure remains the same, and once you have grasped how to make a point secure and how to develop your ideas, you are ready to write on any of the topics you are likely to be asked about. I shall therefore simply give one example of a complicated paragraph, which shows how to compare two characters' views on a theme. Suppose I am answering a question on Shakespeare's *Henry IV Part One*, and I am writing about the theme of honour in the play. Two of the most important characters are Falstaff and Hotspur, and they have strong contrasting ideas about honour. I want to write a paragraph which brings out their different opinions about honour, and highlights the contrast between them. Here is the paragraph I would write:

Falstaff has a cynical attitude to honour, while for Hotspur honour is the highest ideal of his life (**statement**). Falstaff says: 'What is honour?' a word'. To him, the pursuit of honour only leads to death: 'Who hath it? he that died a Wednesday' (**evidence**). Falstaff, then, takes the view that life and pleasures you can physically feel are worth more than an idea like honour which you cannot feel because it is only a 'word' (**developing the idea**). Hotspur says the opposite: when defeated by Hal, he says: 'I better brook the loss of brittle life/Than those proud titles thou hast won of me' (**evidence**). He feels comtempt for life which he describes as 'brittle', and he prefers something he thinks of as higher: ideals of fame or the 'proud titles' which are his honour (**developing the idea**). So their attitudes to honour show us that Falstaff and Hotspur have opposite philosophies: Falstaff will only trust something he can feel, eat or drink; Hotspur, on the other hand, will only admire something he cannot feel, an ideal of honour which he considers to be higher than the everyday facts of life (**developing the two ideas together**).

This is a complicated paragraph because it describes a complex aspect of the play. It is made up of an initial statement, two lots of evidence both followed by development of the idea, and a final part developing the two ideas together. Notice, however, that this paragraph is built up using the same three basic elements which make up a simple paragraph. I have just repeated them as they were needed by the subject-matter and the argument I was developing. Even with more complicated paragraphs, then, be sure to include all three basic elements.

If you write essays in the way I suggest, there is no danger that you will waffle or become irrelevant. Paragraphs along these lines keep you close to the text and ensure that your statements are secure, and give you a sound base for developing more precise and subtle discussion of the text. In the end you will win the case this way, because your essay proves *beyond reasonable doubt* that your understanding of the text is accurate, complex and good.

I have emphasised how important it is to give evidence from the text which supports your point of view. I shall make one last point about this, because one of the most common errors students make in their essays happens when they become so carried away with referring to the text that the whole essay turns into a retelling of the story. You must distinquish between using evidence to support your statements, and this rehashing of what happens, which fails to say anything about the text at all. Retelling the story is a waste of time and loses marks, because the essay does not make any statement and so fails to answer the question. Follow the method I suggest, and your paragraphs will all be based on a statement about the text. Moreover, each statement will be about a topic the question asks you about. The method, then, ensures that your essay steadily and thoroughly develops points which answer the question. Keep to this method, make sure the quotations and references you use are all directly relevant to what you are saying about the text, and you cannot fall into the error of retelling the story.

CONCLUSION

Writing an essay is like making a case in court: you have to bring forward the best evidence and develop a reasoned, logical argument to convince the reader that your understanding of the text is likely to be right. Your evidence is the text you have studied, and you must use the text, in the form of quotations or references, to support statements you make about it. A simple paragraph sets out to make one statement convincingly, and consists of a statement followed by the evidence which supports it, after which you complete the paragraph by developing a more precise and complex idea of the point you want to make. You can do this by asking the question 'Why?' or by comparing statement and evidence. The three elements of such a simple paragraph are the basic elements in all your writing about literature, so to write more complicated paragraphs dealing with more complex points about the text, simply repeat these three elements as your developing argument requires them. But always follow the principles that what you say about the text has to be supported by evidence, and that initial simple statements should be developed as far as possible to reflect the complexity and subtlety of the text.

8

Exam revision and practice

THERE are many different sorts of examinations in Literature; but they have a great deal in common. Whichever particular kind you have to face, the advice in this short chapter should help you. The first part focuses on **revision**: the kind of knowledge to take with you into a literature examination, and the best way of putting it into your head. The second part concentrates on the writing you do in the examination. As in the previous two chapters I assume that the most common form of examination writing is the essay, and suggest planned ways of **practising** so you are ready for the examination.

REVISION

What is tested in a Literature examination? Some factual knowledge, but not much. A few specialised terms, but not many. Some formal technique, but there is no 'syllabus' which forces you to *know* techniques. Most other subjects are different. In English Literature, the only things you **learn** are a few quotations from each of your texts. Nowadays most examining boards allow you to have the text with you, anyway; so even learning quotations is unnecessary. You will already know the specialised terms (like *sonnet, stanza, theme, tragedy, pastoral*) and have techniques, like the methods I have demonstrated in this book; so there is no need to **learn** any of these things. This difference between English Literature and most other subjects is because the Literature examination tests your understanding and response to the complex living world of a text: your judgement, independence, sensitivity; and your ability to think logically under pressure. It is not **learning by rote**.

This is very important, for another reason. You cannot know what questions the examiner will ask or how they will be asked. You may

111

have revised the theme of *education* in Jane Austen's *Pride and Prejudice*, for example; but the examiner asks about the theme of *maturity*. You must be able to realise, in the examination itself, that these are different names for the same theme. Otherwise you will be lost, and think that you cannot answer the question. So, the knowledge you take into the exam must be in an adaptable, flexible form; not rigidly learned off by heart.

Do not **learn** when you revise for Literature, then. On the other hand, Literature revision has to be thorough, and will take up as much of your time as you can give to it. In that case, what should you do? How do you spend all that time, if you are not learning? The answer is to **absorb**. Absorb all the understanding, arguments and ideas, examples of analysis and deduction, that you have gained from studying.

Absorbing

When you have followed a course of study in English Literature, you end up with your essays, with the teacher's comment written at the end of each; a lot of notes you have taken during lessons and when preparing for essays and lessons; and the text. That is the material you now want to absorb. What is in this material? Apart from the text itself, you have amassed ideas, consideration of issues, ways of looking at the text, logical arguments, crisis passages analysed in detail, a teacher's opinion, a classmate's opinion, your own opinion. To absorb this variety, simply sit down somewhere comfortable and read it, but do not make an effort to learn it. Let it come into your mind, but do not try to force it in. Do this repeatedly, starting about three weeks before the day of the examination. Do it more frequently as the day approaches.

Rereading the texts

As for the text itself, you want to reabsorb that as well. Your memory of a text can become hazy, or distorted by distance; and over time you lose any fresh sense of the style and the particular flavour of that text or that writer. You should reread all your texts during the four months before the examination. Treat novels differently because they are much longer: reread any novel you have to revise first, some months early. Then select important episodes from the novel (your crisis episodes will do) to reread again in the hectic final three weeks before the exam. Choose your episodes carefully, making sure (a) that they are spaced through the text, so there is something from near the beginning and something from near the end; and (b) that they deal with the major characters and major themes. Four episodes will be sufficient for most of the novels commonly set.

Reread plays twice: once three months before the examination, and again as late as possible. Plays are a special case because they come alive in the theatre. It is not natural to study them as text and your sense of their dramatic life can quickly fade if you do nothing but analyse them. Yet the examiner may well ask you about 'dramatic effect'. It is not usually possible for you to see your set play the evening before the exam, so the next best thing is to read it through at one, or at most two, sittings. Reading a play only takes as long as performing it: between two and three hours. If you can revive your sense of the play as drama, as a single complete performance, this will be time well-spent. Poetry should also be reread twice at least; but short poems are much easier to fit into a rushed revision timetable, and there is no need to read them all through at once. If, on the other hand, one of your texts is a longer poem (such as Book 1 of *The Prelude* by Wordsworth, or Books 1 and 2 of Milton's *Paradise Lost*), treat it like a play and reread it at one or two concentrated sittings.

The benefits of rereading your texts cannot be exaggerated. You change all the time, so you are likely to notice different things when you read a text again. In addition, there is a powerful process which begins with first reading and study, then allows the text and your understanding of it to mature and expand within you, even though you may concentrate on other work for months. Rereading helps you to recognise the ideas that have matured in you in the meantime. Most students find that their understanding of a text, when they reread it just before the examination, is far more coherent and mature, and more extensive, than it was when they finished studying the same text months earlier. You have matured, your ideas have matured. Capitalise on this process by rereading.

A revision programme

I recommend, then, that you read through your notes and essays repeatedly during the final three weeks, with increasing frequency as the examination approaches; and that you reread your texts about three months before, and again at the last opportunity, sampling long novels by rereading extracts rather than the whole text in the last three weeks. What, then, do you do between three months before, and the final three weeks? During that time you can rewrite your notes, condensing them into as short a form as possible; fill in any gaps in your notes; and make additional new notes that take account of your new, expanded understanding of the texts. This work is not properly called *revision*, however: the aim is to organise your material so you will be able to revise.

The tasks for your final three weeks are repetitive, and you may be revising other subjects where the work seems more urgent because it consists of learning. How can you ensure that you will manage these repetitive revision sessions, with other subjects competing for your time? The only answer is to work out a **revision programme** for yourself, and stick to it. Here is a simple example, worked out for a student who takes a three-hour examination on four set texts, on a Thursday. The texts are *Othello, Pride and Prejudice, The Poems of Thomas Hardy*, and *School for Scandal*.

day	task	time
Wednesday	Read Hardy and *School for Scandal* notes	1.5 hours
	Read 3 Hardy poems	10 mins
Thursday	Read *Othello* and Jane Austen notes	1.5 hours
	Read 3 Hardy poems	10 mins
Friday	Read 10 Hardy poems (at odd times)	30 mins
Saturday	Read *School for Scandal*	2.5 hours
Sunday	Read *School for Scandal* notes	30 mins
Monday	Read Jane Austen episodes	1.5 hours
Tuesday	Read Jane Austen notes	30 mins
	Read 3 Hardy poems	10 mins
Wednesday	Read Hardy and *Othello* notes	1 hour
Thursday	**day off**	–
Friday	Read 10 Hardy poems (at odd times)	30 mins
Saturday	Read *Othello*	2.5 hours
	Read *Othello* notes	30 mins
Sunday	Read 10 Hardy poems and Hardy notes	1 hour
	Read *School for Scandal* notes	30 mins

Monday	**day off**	–
Tuesday	Read all notes	2 hours
	Read Jane Austen episodes	1.5 hours
	Read first and last scenes, *School for Scandal*	30 mins
Wednesday	Read all notes	2 hours
	Read all Hardy poems	1.5 hours
	Read first and last acts of *Othello*	50 mins
Wed. evening or		
Thursday		
morning	Read all notes again	2 hours

This would be an ideal programme, but it is unlikely to be possible because of revision and examinations in other subjects; and because there may be other papers to prepare for your English Literature exam. The three essential principles I have used in constructing this programme, however, should underlie what you do. First, your programme should **begin about three weeks before the exam**. Secondly, you can **check each text in the programme**. For example, I can see I will read my *Othello* notes on Thursday, the following Wednesday, then on Saturday, the next Tuesday and twice through on the final Wednesday. I am satisfied with the number of times I can read them, the spacing, and the increasing frequency. I can check that I will reread *Othello* on the last Saturday, and Acts I and V again the day before the examination. Thirdly, in my programme I **estimate the time I will spend**. It is important to keep the time spent on subjects, and the time spent on different texts, in proportion. Finally, I have included provision for two '**days off**'. These could be juggled to fit my programme in with other commitments, such as examinations in other subjects. They are important because they build flexibility into the programme. However, notice that this programme will allow room for other subjects, not taking up excessive time until the intensive final two days.

The most important advice I can give, however, is to **plan your revision in advance**. Examinations are a stressful time, and it is very easy to fall into the trap of thinking you cannot do any English until after your History examination is over; or concentrating on your favourite text and skimping the others. Because English Literature revision is a process where you **absorb** your understanding, it is vital for you to do it steadily, with controlled increasing intensiveness, over a period of time. You cannot **absorb** in a last-minute rush.

PRACTICE FOR THE EXAMINATION

Timed essays

How do you practise writing essays, so you will be ready to face the strict time-limits imposed in examinations? There is one all-important point to understand in answering this question: **writing an essay is two jobs**. When you write an essay for your course, while you are studying, you are likely to make notes, research the text, write parts of your essay, change your mind, look something up, write more of the essay, and so on. Some months before the examination, you should consciously divide essay-writing into **research and planning** and **writing**.

Your **research and planning** can take as much time as you wish. This part of the work is part of your studying. Later, as the examination itself approaches, it is part of your revision. I can make this clear by asking a plain question: what will happen if you do research in the examination-room? The answer is obvious: disaster. You will not finish the paper. Actually, you do not want to have ideas in the examination. Your job in the examination is to fit ideas you have had before to the questions the examiner happens to ask. **Writing**, on the other hand, must be brought down to the time-limit required by the examination. Begin doing this several months in advance: for all your essays, make sure you finish your research first, then leave a gap, then **write** the essay in a limited, uninterrupted time. I suggest that you start training yourself in this way about six months before the examination. You can begin with a realistic time-limit, and progressively reduce it. By the time of the examination, you should be able to produce essays in the time you will be allowed.

This division of the task into two jobs will also help you to feel more confident. Many students are in the habit of spending several hours on one essay. At university, an essay may take a week. You feel that it is impossible to do the same thing in less than an hour. You are right; but the reassuring answer is that you do not have to. All you have to do in less than an hour is **write** the essay. The method I suggest gives you practice at writing to time; but I have not discussed how to respond to the question quickly, and plan your essays under pressure.

Practise planning essays

You do not want to have ideas in an examination: the ideas should already be there. Writing your essay is not a matter for intensive thought: carry out your plan, paragraph by paragraph, concentrating enough to ensure that your argument is coherent and you use evidence effectively. The most important time in an examination is the first four or five minutes of each answer, the time you spend planning your essay. In these few minutes your mind must work at its peak, analysing the question and designing your answer. If you misread the question, or miss a vital aspect of the subject in your answer, no amount of good writing will regain the marks you have lost. If your plan is good, on the other hand, you can write some clumsy sentences and still obtain a high mark. How can you practise for these sudden bursts of rapid logical thinking?

First, it helps to have a secure method, like the one I explain in Chapter 6. Secondly, you should **practise planning essays** as a separate skill that must be polished in time for the day. Do this by compiling a list of questions about each set text. Look at past examination papers; ask your teacher; find lists of sample questions in study-guides. If you have any difficulty in collecting questions on the text, you can set them for yourself. Make a list of the main characters, the main themes, and any other topics which might be asked about in an examination. Write questions for yourself, copying the style of the examination. This method can never work as well as finding questions from others, however. It is hard to ask yourself questions you are not expecting, so questions from others are likely to give you more realistic practice. You should aim to compile a list of about twenty questions about each of your texts.

The exam is unpredictable, so ask somebody else to select three questions from your list, and copy them on to a separate sheet of paper. Then give yourself a set time in which to produce three plans for essays answering the three questions. I suggest that when you first try this, you should allow forty-five minutes for three plans. Later, reduce this to thirty minutes; and in the final run-up to the examination try to achieve a time of fifteen minutes. Look at Chapter 6 to remind yourself of what a plan should be like. In these practice sessions, however, you can benefit from producing a slightly more elaborate plan.

Write your plan in the same way as described in Chapter 6; then make a note of the textual evidence to use in each paragraph, adding it to the plan. Finally, write your conclusion, your final answer to the question, in the form of one or two clear sentences. Each plan you produce, then, should consist of a list of the main points of your argument in order, with a note of the relevant evidence added to each, and a sentence or two of conclusion. This way of practising essay-plans for the examination is extremely effective and brings other benefits as well. There is a limit to the number of practice essays you can write, as they take too much time. In this way you can face a much larger number of possible questions, forcing your mind to consider the text from a large number of angles. You may chance on the same angle as the examiner uses, of course; but you are bound to increase the flexibility of your thinking, making your mind agile enough to cope with unexpected questions on the day. In addition, the process of choosing relevant evidence to explain such a large number of points makes excellent revision: you become so familiar with the text that you can respond rapidly to any question asked.

CONCLUSION

If you are faced with an examination in English Literature, do not attempt to **learn** facts as you would for other subjects. **Absorb** your knowledge and understanding by repeatedly rereading your notes and essays, and the text. Reread your texts about three months in advance, then organise your notes and fill any gaps. Work out a **revision programme** for the final three weeks before the examination, steadily building up the intensity of your revision towards the final two days. In your revision programme include the time for rereading plays and poetry, and episodes selected from novels, again. To **practise writing**, start six months early by dividing **research** from **writing**, and timing the writing for all essays. Gradually reduce the time allowed until you reach examination time. To **practise planning essays**, collect a list of twenty questions about each of your texts, and write plans to answer them, three at a time, in timed conditions.

9

Taking study further

NATURAL DEVELOPMENTS FROM YOUR STUDY

THIS book has given you a method to rely on when you start to study a literary text. I began at the point where every student faces a feeling of blankness: 'I have read the text, now I am supposed to study it: how do I start?' (see p. 1), and the book sets out to answer that question. The method I have explained takes you far beyond the initial feeling of blankness, but literature study is never 'finished', so there will always be more to discover, and new ways of looking at the text. As you study, the initial approach will become quick and easy, and your mind will naturally seek to explore further. The following discussions indicate three ways in which growing experience and your own mind will push you to take your study further.

1 Between the crises

My method has encouraged you to focus on chosen **crises** from the text and analyse them in detail. This gives you a way of finding the most revealing passages to study first; and it makes sure you focus closely on the text, so that examiners will not complain that your work is 'too generalised'. You will always look at the crises first, however long you continue studying literature. But it will soon be second nature to you: you will do it instinctively with any new text. Then you will want to take your study further.

Remember that a text is like an imagined world, created by the writer as a complete work of art; so everything in the text contributes to the whole. So, the parts of the text **between the crises** are the obvious area to explore when you have the confidence and experience to take things further. Looking between the crises will introduce you to finer distinctions between aspects of themes, characters, style and different ironies; and smaller, more subtle substructures within the overall structure of the text. Just as the crisis throws up clear, strong points, so the rest of the text fills in shades and subtleties with a finer brush.

For example, in Chapter 2 I analysed Elizabeth Bennet from *Pride and Prejudice* by Jane Austen. I examined the crisis when Darcy first proposes to her and found a conflict between society's view that marriage should be about money and social rank, and her own ideal of marriage for love. Here is something Elizabeth says while dancing with Darcy, in Chapter 18 of the novel, long before he has even thought about proposing marriage to her. I have picked it at random by allowing my copy to fall open at any page.

> I have always seen a great similarity in the turn of our minds. We are each of an unsocial, taciturn disposition, unwilling to speak, unless we expect to say something that will amaze the whole room, and be handed down to posterity with all the éclat of a proverb.
>
> (from *Pride and Prejudice*, Penguin, 1972, p. 134)

Elizabeth is teasing Mr Darcy, trying to provoke him. She feels that comparing him with herself will annoy him because she believes him to feel superior. She is also deliberately satirising herself: we know, and she knows, that Elizabeth is talkative, not 'of an unsocial, taciturn disposition, unwilling to speak'. It is a sarcastic strategy, for under cover of this consciously absurd description of herself Elizabeth tells him, to his face, that he is unsocial and taciturn. However, Elizabeth joins this satire to a description of verbal vanity: 'we expect to say something that will amaze the whole room'. In the second half of her sentence, then, she unconsciously describes *her* vanity, the very thing she becomes so ashamed of after the crisis, more than a hundred pages later. Also, the reader is aware that Darcy is treating Elizabeth with unexpected delicacy and politeness. We begin to guess that his heart is softening towards her. So she is probably wrong to think that she will provoke him by pointing out how similar they are. It will not make him angry, but it does go to the centre of the conflict he will later describe, between his growing love for Elizabeth and his sense of the difference in their social positions. Elizabeth's remark, then, must have hurt him in a way she could not imagine. In addition, there is evidence suggesting that Elizabeth already finds Darcy attractive, although she still denies this even to herself. When she says 'I have always seen a great similarity in the turn of our minds', she is thus saying what she impulsively wishes to be the truth, but believes is a sarcastic falsehood. Finally, by the end of the novel we know that there *is* 'a great similarity' in the turn of their minds!

This example shows how many and subtle are the layers of irony and meaning in the text, and how your understanding can become more precise, being modified by details from *between the crises*. Looking at the crisis, I learned that Elizabeth 'was proud of being clever, and vain about being more perceptive than other people'. In the crisis: 'she realises that her vanity has been her undoing' (see p. 35 above). My conclusion was true, but not the whole truth. Now I can be more precise. If Elizabeth were vain about her cleverness, it would matter less. In fact she is vain about showing off her cleverness. She does not 'realise' the whole truth about herself even after the crisis, then. In addition, the way she speaks to Darcy in Chapter 18 shows her partly aware, and self-conscious about her vanity. So the crisis is shaded in with more subtle colours: your understanding becomes more precise and more complex. In this way, by working out through the text from your chosen crises, your understanding will become continuous and connected.

2 Texts throw light on each other

As you gain knowledge of more literary texts, you will find that there are themes that several texts share because writers share the same concerns. Each time this happens you will find it easier to understand the new writer's concerns because you have met them before in another text. Gradually, you build an intuition which enables you to recognise a writer's themes instinctively, making the first steps in studying more rapid. You will also develop another quality, which is difficult to describe. I call it 'wisdom about literature'. It means that you intuitively recognise the great, universal themes of literature. Often, this wisdom enables you to predict how a theme will develop in a book you are just reading for the first time, in the same way as you can predict the ending of a fairy-tale. This effect has already begun to happen, so I shall give an example from texts referred to in this book.

In Chapter 1 I used 'The Tyger' by William Blake to demonstrate finding a theme; and in Chapter 4 I analysed 'Harry Ploughman' by Gerard Manley Hopkins. Blake's poem has a theme of creation, and presents the tiger as fierce and frightening. The poem expresses wonder at the contrasts and variety in creation. Looking at the world gave Blake a feeling of fear, beauty and awe, which led to an intense moment of enlightenment when he appreciated the unlimited power and wisdom of the Creator. The poem expresses this intense revelation. 'Harry Ploughman' is a very different poem, but the writer's feelings are surprisingly similar. He sees the rough strength of the ploughman which, in a moment of illumination, is transformed into delicate beauty because the poet suddenly appreciates how all things – even contrasting things – work together to produce the world's beauty. As you read and study more widely, you will recognise variations on this theme in the work of many great writers. Really, both of these poets see things that don't seem to fit together (tiger and lamb; Harry's roughness and his grace). It is a common experience to feel baffled by violence or evil, and love and beauty, in the world; and everyone at some time in their lives tries to make sense of it all, hoping to find purpose behind what seems destructive or chaotic. If you are familiar with the novels of Thomas Hardy, you can recognise the same bafflement and desire for a sign of divine purpose in the way his characters endure painful shocks, and moments of happiness, in life. Hardy's conclusion, however, is pessimistic.

Your growing experience of literature will accelerate all aspects of your studying. Think back to Chapter 4, when I discussed imagery in *Romeo and Juliet*. I explained that imagery often works by connecting the **particular** with the **universal**, so Romeo's image for Juliet connects one young Veronese girl with the universal life-giving properties of the sun. Soon, you will recognise the significance of **universal** imagery instinctively. Without thinking, you will understand the seasons, the agricultural year, day and night, youth and age, and numerous other references which recur in English Literature texts. They make a recurring pattern of meaning which you can interpret in an instant. So, when Thomas Hardy writes that Time:

> . . . shakes this fragile frame at eve
> With throbbings of noontide.
> (from *Chosen Poems of Thomas Hardy*, Macmillan, 1975, p. 87)

you know that he is an old man shaken by a young man's passions, because 'eve' (i.e. 'evening') = old age, and 'noontide' = the prime of life. The instant recognition of universal imagery will enhance your pleasure in reading, bringing a richer understanding as you read texts for the first time.

As you continue to study, your mind will realise connections between texts you have read and those you are reading for the first time. You will come across many examples of universal imagery, become familiar with major literary themes such as appearance and reality, order and disorder, reason and passion, idealism and disillusion, education (or maturity), and love. This growth of experience and understanding has a cumulative effect, making your study increasingly satisfying and progressively richer in rewards.

3 Beyond 'the text as a whole'

Your thoughts about the text will move on of their own accord, beyond the end of Step 3. Remember that our method of study relies on asking and answering leading questions based on what you already know. This makes you think logically and analytically, and as you gain experience it will become a habit. Soon, your mind will automatically pose further leading questions at the end of Step 3, without having to be prompted.

What kinds of questions will take you beyond Step 3? At the end of our method, remember, you have related your understanding of details in the text (*'the part you have studied'*) to the whole text. The next step is to ask: how does this whole text relate to other texts / to the form in which it is written / to the historical development of literature / to cultures / to ideas? These questions are a natural progression, and will take you into a range of larger subjects and issues. In particular, you can consider the text as an original work of art. What are its special qualities? What makes this text or this writer unique, what does it contribute to the form? Also, think about what kind of work it is, starting with the **genre** (novel, play, poem) and going on to less obvious differences between writers and works. How, for example, does a nineteenth-century work of social realism such as Dickens's *Hard Times* differ from an eighteenth-century gothic work such as Mrs Radcliffe's *The Mysteries of Udolpho*? What do they have in common that makes us call them both 'novels'? Or, why do we call Jane Austen's *Pride and Prejudice* a 'novel of manners' but Virginia Woolf's *To the Lighthouse* a 'psychological novel'? The medium of exploration and revelation is manners in one, and psychological in the other, perhaps. Is this because people changed the way they think about themselves, or have people changed the way they *are*, between Jane Austen's eighteenth century and Virginia Woolf's twentieth century?

EXPERTS AND EXPERTISE

The critics

Throughout this book I have focused on the text itself and advised you to avoid the confusing influence of professional literary critics, books about books. Remember that your own response to literature, and your own understanding of a text, is as valid as any expert's. Literature is about ordinary life, and you know as much about living as anyone else. It is important to remember this advice, and remain confident of the validity of your own judgement, when you pursue your study to a higher level and you are expected to read the critics.

Read them critically. Look at their analysis and the conclusions they draw from the text. Accept those which are reasonable, but disagree when they are not reasonable, when you think they are wrong. All the time, remember that it is possible to share being right: the experts are only individuals, and they and you may respond to a writer in different ways which are all part of the truth.

To see how this can happen, remember finding a theme in Chapter 1, and think about Emily Brontë's *Wuthering Heights* again. I noticed that the novel is a love story, that the plot revolves around marriages, affairs and betrayals of love; so I chose to study the theme of love. This led me to conclusions about love as a force more powerful than life or death, and I found a number of other insights on the way. What if I were not interested in love? What if I were interested in society on the day when I started to study *Wuthering Heights*? Then, I would notice that the Earnshaws' farm is wild and primitive and their behaviour violent, expressing unrestrained emotions. Their religion, represented by the old servant Joseph, emphasises punishment and God's anger. Their idea of justice is revenge. In contrast, the Lintons live in a civilised house in a sheltered valley, surrounded by a tame 'park'. They have sophisticated manners and hide their feelings, and the emphasis in their religion is on God's love and mercy; the Lintons' justice is fairness and balance, not revenge. While the Earnshaws work with their hands on the farm, the Lintons do not work, but use their education, being landowners and magistrates. If I noticed these features of *Wuthering Heights*, I would choose to study the theme of social conflict between different classes. My analysis would lead to completely different conclusions from those I reached after studying the theme of love. My conclusions would be just as **true**, and just as **valid**, as those about love. Their difference would reflect the difference in me when I chose a theme.

Professional critics often disagree with each other. They sometimes argue with each other in their books, demolishing each other's arguments and making scathing comments. This can be very confusing for the student, unless you know that most of their disagreements only mirror a very common-sense truth: what you get out of literature is bound to reflect who you are, and what interests you bring to it in the first place.

It follows naturally that most professional criticism is good criticism, and it can stimulate your study. It is good when it is skilful, enlightening analysis of the text; and it can stimulate you for the very simple reason that it is somebody else's view. It will often bring you ideas that you would never have thought of for yourself. This is not because critics are cleverer than students. They may be, but that is not the point. It is because the student is not the critic and the critic is not the student. It is a pity that many students of literature have few opportunities to discuss their texts with other people. A good argument about a book can give you the same stimulation as reading a critic: your friend will challenge your ideas, forcing you to justify what you say and prove your point from the text; and they will put forward their ideas, which would not have occurred to you. Treat professional critics just as you would a friend who is putting a different view from your own. Test their ideas to make sure they can justify them from the text. Never give up your own point of view, but think about it critically and measure its worth against the new angle which had not occurred to you. It is most important to keep in mind this clear distinction: there is a right way and a wrong way to use 'expert' views. Never follow them slavishly, obliterating your own understanding of the text. On the other hand, do take them in and build on them to enlarge and enrich your understanding.

I have said that the expert critics' views vary because they are different people. You should also be warned that some of them bring a complete, ready-made theory to every text: their ideas are worked out in detail before they start to analyse. There are many of these preconceived ideas, which often contradict each other. They are called **lit-erary theories** or **schools of criticism**, and you will come to know the most influential ones as you continue to study. For example, there is something called **Marxist criticism** and something else called **Structuralism**. Briefly, the Marxist critic always comes to a text bringing with him Marx's theory of historical inevitability and struggles between social classes. Most English literature has been written by the middle or bourgeois class, and the Marxist critic will often analyse the text in order to explore the bourgeois – that is the author's – perception of society, class and history. Thus, it is of great interest to a Marxist critic that the only non-bourgeois scene we witness in all Jane Austen's novels is Fanny's visit to Portsmouth in *Mansfield Park*. Fanny is the heroine and was taken from relative poverty when a child. After years of bourgeois comfort, she is shocked and repelled by visiting her native class, and her bourgeois aspirations are reinforced. The Marxist critic will be fascinated by this aspect of the text, and point to the power of social class over Fanny, who almost marries against her con-science in order to escape the shock of poverty. The **Structuralist**, on the other hand, will have nothing to do with history, society and class. These are concepts the Structuralist deliberately avoids in order to focus on the internal pattern or 'grammar' of the text. You can find clear, readable explanations of these literary theories in John Peck and Martin Coyle's *Literary Terms and Criticism: A Student's Guide* (Macmillan, 1984). It is not within the scope of this book to explain literary theories, however, so I shall finish with some brief advice on how to think about them.

A literary text is like a world. It is limited, in comparison to the chaotic complexity of real life; but it is complex and constructed with numerous facets. Critics who follow a **literary theory** deliber-ately focus on one part of this world of the text, because their theory tells them it is more significant than anything else. Imagine, then, two spacemen looking at Earth. One sees the oceans but is blind to the land. The other sees continents but is blind to the oceans. The first says 'See! a blue planet!', and the second says 'Ah! Such wondrous browns and greens!' It will not be long before they argue, accusing each other of blindness. Yet, if we can only see what both of them see, we will appreciate the world as a whole! Understand the theories of literature, then. They have a contribution to make, and can be enlightening, but they can also be blind to each other's perceptions.

Information from outside the text

You will find there is a large amount of information available to help you study a text. There are a lot of points you can look up in your edition or in reference books, and there is a lot of extra material you can read, all designed to make you better informed. It is worth dividing all this extra information into two kinds, because it gives two different kinds of help. First, there are notes in your edition of the text, dictionaries, and so on, which help you with **the actual meaning of the text**. Secondly, there is information which tells you about the authors' lives and times, their views, and other points which are supposed to affect your **interpretation of a text**. I recommend that you make free use of the first kind whenever you want to; but avoid the second kind until you have developed your own response quite a long way, through your own study.

It is necessary to understand the **actual meaning** of what you read. Suppose you are studying Shakespeare's *Hamlet*, and you read this in Hamlet's first soliloquy:

> O, that this too too solid flesh would melt,
> Thaw, and resolve itself into a dew!
> Or that the Everlasting had not fix'd
> His canon 'gainst self-slaughter! O God! God!
> How weary, stale, flat, and unprofitable,
> Seem to me all the uses of this world!
> Fie on't! Ah, fie! 'tis an unweeded garden,
> That grows to seed; things rank and gross in nature
> Possess it merely. That it should come to this!
> But two months dead! nay, not so much, not two.
> So excellent a king that was to this
> Hyperion to a satyr . . .
>
> (*Hamlet*, I.ii.129–40, *The Complete Works*, Collins, 1964)

You are uncertain about some of the words in this speech. 'Canon', for example, is not part of the artillery; you have not heard anyone exclaim 'Fie!'; and you have not come across 'merely' used in this strange way. Most editions of *Hamlet* will answer two of your questions at the bottom of the page in the form of a note. 'Canon' is a *law* in the Signet Shakespeare, and a *divine decree* in the New Variorum edition; and 'merely' is given as *entirely* and *completely* respectively. My dictionary tells me that 'Fie!' is *an exclamation expressing disgust or reproach*. In the same extract Hamlet mentions 'Hyperion' and 'a satyr' as similes for his father the old king and his uncle the new king. My editions of the play help me again: the Signet Shakespeare gives 'Hyperion' as *the sun god, a model of beauty*, but fails to tell me what a 'satyr' is. The New Variorum gives a ten-line note on 'Hyperion' discussing five scholars' views on spelling and accent on the name. Then there is a four-line note on 'to a satyr', which is about scholars arguing over grammar; and a five-line note about 'satyr', complaining that one scholar thought one thing but another thought not. By this time students who want to know what a satyr is will be so irritated they will run to their Dictionary of Mythology and discover that satyrs were lazy, useless and sensual half-human half-monkey-and-goat creatures from Greek mythology. Now, at last (and with no help from editors of Shakespeare!) you understand that Hamlet compares the finest and worst of mythological figures to his father and uncle respectively.

The point is that you need this kind of information so you can **understand what Hamlet says**. It clarifies the meaning of the words, without influencing the way you respond to the text. Look up anything you do not understand in this way, as soon as you start to study a text.

The second kind of information provided for you is not needed until you have read and studied the text. It can distort your response because it is difficult to be open and objective if your mind is cluttered with outside information. Avoid it, then, for the same reason as you should avoid reading critics until you have reached an advanced stage in your own study. The poem 'Harry Ploughman', which was discussed in Chapter 4, makes an excellent example of the virtue of studying for yourself first, and the danger of reading outside information too soon.

I used 'Harry Ploughman' to demonstrate analysing a poem by looking at the imagery. I did not refer to outside information. Remember the conclusion I reached:

The poet is not moved by the fact that the plough hurls earth. He is moved by the creation of shining beauty, which is expressed by the **image** for the earth, 'With-a-fountain's shining-shot furls'. Also, I found that the imagery is in contrasting groups: solid, liquid; hard, soft. This helps me to understand the odd word Hopkins has invented, 'Churls-grace'. A churl is a peasant and our impression is of a rough and earthy person, in contrast to 'grace' which brings to mind elegance, delicacy and also (in its religious sense) God's love. Putting the contrasts of imagery and the meaning together, then, tells me that the poem is about the way contrasting things can be brought together and work together to produce shining beauty. The images of an army unit and 'one crew' emphasise this point. (above, p. 80)

Hopkins is a 'difficult' poet; his poems look hard to understand and he invents his own words (like 'Churlsgrace' in 'Harry Ploughman'), so students approaching his poetry often lose confidence and look for help. Teachers, study-guides or critical works respond. Hopkins students are then in an even worse situation. Not only do they have to wrestle with 'difficult' poetry; they are also ordered to wrestle with *sprung rhythm*, Hopkins's own original meter; and with *inscape* and *instress*, Hopkins's theory of God's presence through nature, developed from classical philosophy and medieval theology. The student looks at the poems and cries 'Help!' Teachers and critics eagerly provide all this extra information, which makes matters worse. Here is an extract from one of the best explanations of *inscape* and *instress* I have found. As you read it, ask yourself: would this have helped me understand 'Harry Ploughman' if I could not understand it for myself?

> Hopkins is mainly fascinated by those aspects of a thing, or *group* of things, which constitute its individual and 'especial' unity of being, its 'individually-distinctive beauty', or (if 'beauty' is not involved) the very essence of its nature. For this unified pattern of essential attributes (often made up of various sense-data) he coined the word 'inscape'; and to that energy or stress of being which holds the 'inscape' together he gave the name 'instress'. This 'instress' is often referred to as the force which also, as an impulse *from* the 'inscape', carries it whole into the mind of the perceiver.
> (from *The Poems of Gerard Manley Hopkins*, eds Gardner and Mackenzie, OUP, 1967, p. xx)

This is the easier part of the editors' discussion of 'inscape' and 'instress'. The next page refers to ancient and medieval philosophers and traces the development of Hopkins's two ideas from what he studied. I shall simplify 'inscape' and 'instress' for you, because I want you to compare Hopkins's philosophical ideas with the conclusion I reached about 'Harry Ploughman' without their help.

Everything God created is itself. So, a ploughman is a ploughman, designed for, skilled at, *made for* ploughing. Sometimes things express themselves perfectly. For example, if you see a ploughman ploughing, you see him being perfectly himself. You see perfect skill, grace, coordination. Everything is 'right' about him. *Inscape* is the name Hopkins gave to the 'rightness' of things being themselves. When you see 'inscape' it gives you a feeling: admiration, or a sudden pleasure. You appreciate what you see intensely. Hopkins thought of this as a kind of energy which travels from the *inscape* to you, as you are watching. He called this *instress*. In very brief terms, when you see *inscape*, you feel *instress*.

What did I discover from studying 'Harry Ploughman'? I said that 'the poet is moved by the creation of shining beauty'; and that 'the poem is about the way contrasting things can be brought together and work together to produce shining beauty'. In fact, I understood 'inscape' (Harry's strength and perfect coordination when ploughing) and 'instress' (the poet's wondering response, expressed in bright images: which is also, obviously, the energy which made him write the poem) just from studying the text. Afterwards, when I read the **outside information**, I gained new jargon names for ideas I already understood. What would have happened if I worked the other way around? What if I read about 'inscape' and 'instress' first? I would have been so confused before reading the poem that it would have been very hard work to make any sense of it at all.

This example demonstrates the importance of starting with the text itself, even when you have much more experience at studying. If you begin by understanding 'Harry Ploughman', it is quite easy to understand about 'inscape' and 'instress', and you will be able to make use of the information to take your ideas further; but if you begin with the **outside information**, there is a real danger that your own understanding will be distorted or sabotaged, or at least made much more difficult.

CONCLUSION

As you take studying further, you will increase the subtlety of your understanding by studying between the crises you first look at; you will find how texts throw light on each other when they have similar themes and you will recognise the great universal themes and patterns of imagery. You will ask leading questions which take you beyond Step 3 of our method. You will also make use of the world of professional literature study by reading the critics, learning about literary theories, and using scholarly information about texts and authors. Two principles should guide you in your contact with this professional world of literary studies. First, your own response is as valid as anyone else's; so you must always be critical of experts' views. Secondly, you must always study the text first, reaching at least our Step 3 before looking at critics or other information. The only exception to this second principle is for the kind of information which helps you to understand the actual meaning of the text. And do remember to enjoy yourself.

Further reading

As I said in the last chapter, an enormous number of critical books and essays have been written about every author or text you are likely to study. I discussed the question: are these critical books worth reading? The answer is, yes, they often are, but be very careful how you handle them. There are three cardinal points which will have come across clearly from the whole of this book, and my discussion in Chapter 9. The first is that there is no substitute for doing your own work on a text. If you simply borrow ideas from critical books your essays will appear sterile and second-hand, and of course you will be no better at reading the literature itself afterwards than you were before. The second point is that there must be a direct link between your views and the evidence which supports them in all your essays, as I stressed in Chapter 7. Doing your own work on the text is the surest way to prepare for writing convincing, successful essays. Finally, studying the text for yourself makes you the professional critic's equal: you can compare his or her views with your own. For these reasons I recommend that you take it as a rule not to read any critical books about the text you are studying until you have finished studying it for yourself.

The warning about evidence in essays applies particularly to 'study-guides' on set authors and texts. Some of these merely summarise the text and give potted, unexplained views of the main themes and characters. 'Potted' views are no use in an essay because they are not supported by your analysis of the text, so if you rely on such guides your essays will be unconvincing and out of touch. Finally, not all critics are good at their work. Some quite ridiculous views are published. It really is simpler, safer and much more rewarding to select passages from a text yourself and get down to the business of analysing those passages and relating them to the text as a whole. That is the way that anyone who is good at English goes about it, and there is really no alternative approach. It is also, as I pointed out in Chapter 9, the easiest and most natural way to gain an understanding of the text, and will keep you clear of the distortions and confusions some critics and 'expert' information could cause.

I do want to recommend some reading in this final section, however. It should hardly need saying that the best way to find out about literature is to read a lot of books, but it is also true to say that students beginning to develop an interest in books and who are keen to read often find the sheer volume and variety of English Literature baffling and daunting. It may prove useful, then, if I provide a short list. As regards novels I suggest you try Jane Austen's *Pride and Prejudice*, Charles Dickens's *Great Expectations*, Thomas Hardy's *The Mayor of Casterbridge* and D. H. Lawrence's *Sons and Lovers*. Obviously you can add to this list quite easily, as you can to the following list of plays: Shakespeare's *Twelfth Night, Hamlet* and *The Tempest*, R. B. Sheridan's *The Rivals*, Arthur Miller's *Death of a Salesman* and Harold Pinter's *The Caretaker*.

Poetry presents a special problem. If I simply list poets you will face volumes of verse, and each volume will contain upwards of a hundred poems. Instead I have chosen some actual poems which you can try. I think these are good examples which represent the particular poet's work, but of course I hope you will read more afterwards. Try John Donne's 'The Sunne Rising' and 'A Valediction: Forbidding Mourning', Alexander Pope's 'The Rape of the Lock', Coleridge's 'The Ancient Mariner', Wordsworth's 'Tintern Abbey', Gerard Manley Hopkins's 'The Windhover', Thomas Hardy's 'The Voice' and 'The Darkling Thrush', and Yeats's 'The Wild Swans at Coole' and 'Sailing to Byzantium'. You could perhaps read more widely in twentieth-century poetry, and try poems by T. S. Eliot, W. H. Auden, Robert Graves, Dylan Thomas and Ted Hughes.

Looking back over my list I can see that it is already quite daunting, and at the same time I am aware of the large number of authors I have left out. However, if you look on this list as a sort of companion and not as a programme, and if you start reading for enjoyment and not as a duty, you will find that you will begin to establish a confident sense of the nature of English Literature and also that you may well have found a new source of pleasure in life.